Cork Literary Review

Cork Literary Review
Volume VII

Edited by Eugene O'Connell

Assistant Editor
Liz Willows

bradshaw books
Cork

First published in 2000 by

bradshaw books
Tigh Filí (Poets' House)
Thompson House
MacCurtain Street
Cork, Ireland
Phone 353 21 4509274
Fax 353 21 4551617
e-mail admin@cwpc.ie
Website http://www.tighfili.com

© The Authors

British Library Cataloguing in Publication Data
ISBN 0 949010 70 7

Cover Batik by Ruth Holmes
Cover design by Nick Sanquest
Typeset and Layout at Tigh Filí
Printed and Bound by Techman, Dublin

The contemplation of things as they are,
without error or confusion,
without substitution or imposture,
is in itself a nobler thing
than a whole harvest of invention.

Francis Bacon

Acknowledgements

A special word of thanks to Liz Willows, Managing Editor and Literature Officer at Tigh Filí, for her excellence and dedication to this project. To Aisling Lyons for her research and compilation of biographical details and her typing and proofreading; Breda Foran for her preparation of copy for screen; Nick Sanquest who designed our cover and proofread portions of text; and to all the staff at Tigh Filí for their enterprise and committment.

Contents

Editorial

In his autobiography of life on the Great Blasket, Tomás Ó Criomthainn recalls how he went to the hill one day to cut turf and was waylaid by the island poet Dunleavy, who persuaded him to "fish out pencil and paper" to take down the many verses of the poem 'The Blackfaced Sheep'. The reluctant scribe recalls afterwards that not only had he idled away the day on this useless enterprise but that when he went to eat his packed lunch "a horse couldn't have champed the hunk of yellow bread and my milk had turned to stone". Yet on the cover of *An tOileánach*, his memoir of island life, Tomás is pictured holding his book as if it were some sort of revered icon whose word recorded for posterity the life of a people whose like would not be seen again: "Ní bheidh a leithéidí arís ann".

Though he was a practical man well used to the harsh realities of life and death on his island home, he realised the necessity for his generation and each succeeding one to interpret itself through its art and literature, or as Chekhov put it: "to add ascetic or finer arts to its professional and commercial interests". We live in a country that wants for little and yet Ó Criomthainn's words were never more relevant and have formed the guiding principle behind my selection of interviews, articles and comment, in this the last of the three books I have been asked to edit. I was privileged to work with David Marcus, Bernard O'Donoghue, the writers and poets who have contributed to the book and to the competitions, and of course Máire Bradshaw, the publisher and guiding light behind the *Cork Literary Review*.

Eugene O'Connell

Dennis O'Driscoll: A Promise Fulfilled
in conversation with **Eugene O'Connell**

Dennis O'Driscoll was born in Thurles on the first of January in 1954. He grew up in Mill Road on the outskirts of the 'anonymous' town that boasted the Bishop's Palace, Priests' training college, sugar factory and Hayes' Hotel (where the GAA was founded): all the spiritual and secular icons of the Saorstat, the official Ireland of its day.

He remembers his childhood town as a place imbued with a wonder that is more than nostalgia and redolent of Wordsworth's Cumbria where he experienced the first intimations of his own mortality.

There were lighter moments like the inappropriately named 'New Cinema' advertising some film under the banner "last showing in Ireland"; the infamous "No cursing, by order of the committee" sign, that stood behind the goalposts in Kickham Park; and the advice he received at the local Christian Brothers' School to: "Marry a girl beneath your station – she'll rise to your level".

Dennis opted for the Junior Ex. exam as the wisest of the three career options (the other two being teacher training or emigration), available at the time and joined the Civil Service at the age of sixteen. He is now Assistant Principal Officer in the Customs Division in South Castle Street in Dublin, where he co-ordinates EU and Irish Customs Law.

At the young age of twenty-three he was already writing for magazines like *Hibernia* and had his first poems published in *Poetry Australia*.

The early death of his parents in their fifties was to have a profound influence on his early collections such as *Kist*, with its passionate outrage at the seemingly indiscriminate visitation of pain and death on their young lives. The twin themes of suffering and fatalism in the face of death, are constant in his work.

Unlike a previous generation of writers like Hugh Leonard, who left the stifling routine of The Department of Lands to become a full time writer, O'Driscoll embraced the clinical mindset of the Civil Service, using it as a vehicle to explore and criticise contemporary poetry. He also acknowledges the profound influence of poet/civil servants like Thomas Kinsella, Philip Larkin and Wallace Stephens.

1

Eugene O'Connell

In Miroslav Holub, the Czech poet and immunologist, he found a kindred spirit whose search for meaning mirrored his own metaphysical temperament and whose advocacy of poetry as a hobby/vocation allowed O'Driscoll to accommodate his passion for poetry into his day job.

In a celebrated essay on Eastern European poetry in *The Cambridge Quarterly* he sets out his own vision when he denounces the trivia of modern English verse and claims it doesn't, in the end, take the measure of both the awe of existence and the value of one individual life as Eastern European poets like Holub do, or as the Elizabethan poets did in the passion of their individual address to society.

One senses that the passionate outrage, the more matter than art, of the earlier collections like *Kist* and *Hidden Extras* have become something of an embarrassment to the sober civil servant of later years whose instinct to measure and quantify sees emotional display as suspect and exploitative of the sensibilities of his audience.

In his recent and highly praised collections like *Quality Time* and *Weather Permitting* (winner of last year's prestigious Lannon Award), he has moved from the 'confessional mode' which he suspects of exploiting personal and private grief, to the 'analytic mode' of a poet like Holub, who will dissect his subject and allow the reader to construct his own poem from the parts.

He has anchored much of his recent work in the mundane world of his Civil Service workplace and has become labelled 'the office poet' for memorable sequences like *The Bottom Line* whose series of sonnets explore the different states of consciousness of the individual in his everyday workplace who realises:

> Then the time comes when you know
> none of your promise will be fulfilled;
> the saving roles luck, fame, deliverance
> from your job were meant to play...
> You will slave on till pension day,
> eluded by advancement, satisfaction, wealth.
>
> In your head, some plangent melody repeats;
> in your mind's eye, a preview of your part
> as walk-on stoic, accepting failure in good
> heart, battling home against the wind
> this night the same as the last.

Dennis O'Driscoll's double life as a civil servant and poet/critic has enabled him to subject modern poetry to the rigorous acid-test of an outside independent agency. He agrees with Craig Raine that poets don't necessarily have a monopoly on pain any more than others do and with Richard Murphy, "that the mere ambition" to write a poem can often be enough to kill it.

A scrupulously honest critic, he challenges our preconceived notions of poetry and poets. His varied and eclectic snatches and quotes in his 'Pickings and Choosings' column in *Poetry Ireland Review* illustrate his tough-minded but always democratic approach to his beloved craft.

> It's an immense discipline for a poet to work among people who think nothing of literature, and after all, if poetry is about anything, it's about the same world that other people live in   *C.H. Sisson*

> Virtue and poetry are not synonymous   *Charles Simic*

> I think for a poet the struggle from the beginning is to really find the confidence and authority of your own voice, not only in terms of style but how to get to the point where what you're writing on the page is, metrically and in terms of the tone, the exact voice in which you speak   *Derek Walcott*

> In Estonian, the lovely word for 'poet' – luuletaja – also means liar   *Sally Laird*

> I wish I could open a magazine now with the same excitement with which I once opened *Nimbus* to find a Kavanagh   *John McGahern*

> I like the company of poets. They take you away from the boring realities of life, if you like, and open up all sorts of new exciting things, sometimes quite startling   *Charles J. Haughey*

Dennis O'Driscoll

Either

They are somewhere in the world, pouring soya milk
on porridge during the dream-time before work,
        or sprouting thick fungal whiskers
in a graveyard's penetrating damp –
the ones I used to know, with whom I lost
touch, who were once the mainstay of my
        gossip; squash partners, office colleagues,
obnoxious neighbours, friends of friends.

As I speak they scrutinise the milk carton's text
or subside more comfortably into sleep
        that resurrection's long-haul wait entails
our paths crossed then grassed over again.
They are either alive and well or decomposing
slowly in a shroud; I could either call them up
        and chat, or confirm that they are ex-directory now.
It is a matter of life and death.

A Voice that Needs to be Heard

Barbara Brown looks at the evolution of Dennis O' Driscoll's long poem, *The Bottom Line*

On the first of January 2000, Thurles-born Dennis O'Driscoll celebrated not only the first day of the new millennium but also his forty-sixth birthday. He had, and has, good reason to celebrate. Already well-regarded as a poet and critic of poetry in Ireland, Britain, America and Australia, in October he was one of the recipients (with Louise Gluck and Adrienne Rich) of the prestigious Lannan Literary Award for Poetry, a $75,000 grant from the Lannan Foundation, Santa Fe, New Mexico. Last November in Dublin, Anvil Press launched his book of poetry, *Weather Permitting*.

Reviewers and interviewers continue to emphasise O'Driscoll's 'double life', his dual roles as poet/critic and Dublin civil servant for more than sixty years. Long successful in both careers, O'Driscoll, after completing his Leaving Certificate at sixteen years old, entered the Office of the Revenue Commissioners. For him, as for Philip Larkin, it was an inspired choice, anchoring him in the world and providing him with a social life and a world-language, yet allowing him to keep imaginative space for his private life. In 1977, at twenty-three, his first poems were published by poet Les Murray in *Poetry Australia*, and his first poetry reviews appeared in *Hibernia*. The poems were followed by four books of poetry: *Kist*, 1982; *Hidden Extras*, 1987; *Long Story Short*, 1993; and *Quality Time*, 1997. Also published in 1997 was *As the Poet Said...Poetry Pickings and Choosings*, edited by poet Tony Curtis. O'Driscoll's essays, both autobiographical and critical, and his reviews, have been published in the *TLS*, *Harvard Review*, *Paris Review* and the *London Magazine*. He has been influential in bringing critical attention to Eastern European writers such as Miroslav Holub and Marina Tsvetayeva. Ironically his poetry has seldom been the subject of academic papers or studies. One exception is his admitted favourite, the long poem, *The Bottom Line* (hereafter cited as *TBL*). In *TBL*, O'Driscoll's two careers reach a creative symbiosis.

Originally published in a limited edition in 1994 and then revised as 'Part Two' of *Quality Time*, *TBL* is a poem in 50 eleven-line stanzas. The lines are unrhymed. The poem is largely iambic, but does include ten and twelve-syllable lines, and fewer. The sonnets are free-form, such as we've seen in the poetry of George Meredith and e.e. cummings, among others. It is, as Robert Haas suggests, "Shakespeare's meter at the end of the 20th century". Neither a narrative nor a fiction and not ordered chronologically, the 'I' of the poem represents a montage of nameless individuals, all male, with their diverse personalities, attitudes and perspectives. O'Driscoll's portrayal – detached, objective, yet sympathetic – balances positive as well as negative aspects of their materialistic lives at work and at home, where they enjoy 'quality time'.

O'Driscoll's dual careers enable him to shape in *TBL* a non-traditional subject, the contemporary world of the office, into a poem "that didn't flinch from treating business people as a legitimate, even important, subject for contemporary poetry". As O'Driscoll further explained to interviewer and poet Isabelle Cartwright: "The reality is that there are millions of us heading into these sort of buildings every day and nobody much in literature pays attention to us here" (*Cobweb*, 30). His career as civil servant familiarised him with the language of the office, with its ambition-fired environment and superficial relationships, and led him to believe that, "Offices are a kind of paradigm or model for the outside". His talent as a writer prepared him to transmute the prosaic language of the bureaucratic and business worlds of the 1980s and 90s into poetry.

For over ten years O'Driscoll had produced a series of poems which thematically foreshadow *TBL*. 'BLOCKING A POST', published in *Poetry Ireland* in 1982, is a monologue spoken by a complacent civil servant completely dependent upon routine and precedent:

> I have signed the attendance book and started work
> at the same time every morning for decades...

He is smug in his determination to control each moment:

> The one chance element in my life is death,
> The only unprovided-for contingency.

But the voice is never fully convincing, the ten, four-line stanzas choppy, the language prose-y and flat. O'Driscoll considers it a failed attempt, yet it is significant as an initial impulse to recreate the world of the bureaucrat.

In his first book, *Kist*, published the same year, the poem 'Death Duties' employs a more successful voice and persona who passes:

routine, duplicated days, working on Death Duties,
where my initials stand for "date of death" on files,
and "I.R.A." means Inland Revenue Affidavit.

Hidden Extras, 1987, has four descriptions of the workaday world – 'Office Photograph', 'Man Going to the Office', 'At the Top', and 'Serving Time' – written in a variety of poetic forms and structures, and highlighting O'Driscoll's gift of creating memorable phrases from this dull setting. A voice in 'At the Top' declares, "Wars, shortages, strikes can all be put to use"; the anonymous narrator in 'Serving Time' states, "I am undisputed Lord of the Files".

Two poems from *Long Story Short*, 1993, 'In Office' and 'Midnight Oil' sustain this thematic progression. Each of the four stanzas of 'In Office' opens with a strident third person plural narrative voice; the rhythm is militant, jarring:

We are marching for work...
We forego identity and drive...
Work is the nightmare from which we yearn to wake...
We age in the mirrors of office lavatories...

Of most interest, however, is 'Midnight Oil', with its ironic title and obvious reference to the cliché 'burning the midnight oil'. The poem is set in 'high-rise offices' where:

the struggle which takes place
is, to the pained occupant
of the swivel chair,
a matter of profit or loss
– in other words, life or death.

'Midnight Oil' was for O'Driscoll a breakthrough, an 'aura' poem, in which he focuses on commonplace things, trivial and seemingly unpoetic, in a style and tone close to the vignettes of *TBL*. Although the poem's shortened lines restrict a full development of its subject, its cryptic language moves towards the 'business-speak' of the fully developed sequence to follow.

O'Driscoll's account of the genesis of *TBL* is instructive:

Barbara Brown

I never said to myself, "Now I am going to write a long poem" or "I'll write an office poem". What happened was that I wrote one eleven-line poem about visiting the supermarket where there was a mirror at the cash register. I was shocked to see myself looking like a bureaucrat taking my credit card out of my wallet. It was one of those moments when you realise that you have grown up, that you had conformed, that you have become so much part of a world that you didn't expect to become part of. You don't expect to be that integrated into the slightly alien world of middle management and all that. So, the first eleven-line stanza didn't seem complete, it needed another and so on until there were sixty. Then I abolished ten including the original one about the supermarket. (*Cobweb*, 29-30)

He adds:

I know that the way to write a long poem is not to try to write a long poem.

Previously unpublished drafts of O'Driscoll's first two eleven-line stanzas establish the form of *TBL*. Still earlier drafts of these poems, titled 'SELF-PORTRAITS' were of varying lengths:

SELF-PORTRAITS

I
It takes more than a minute
To recognise the bleary customer
Reflected near the check-out,
Accumulating meat and low-fat spreads.
I go on to sign the credit card slip,
Wheel the trolley under cavernous concrete,
Expect my parents to swoop down
And announce my game is up.
I help them load the grocery bags,
Then squeeze into the back seat
For the tense drive home.

II
The kind of double-breasted suit
a Nineties man must wear;
turn-ups on the trousers,
the right space between the stripes
of the grey shirt; subtle after-shave...
Problems which occupy me now,
struggling with pre-meeting notes,
will pass away like fashions:
funny collars, floral ties
my grandchildren will scoff at
when albums do the rounds.

O'Driscoll recognised in stanza II the tone which will inform *TBL* and abandoned the 'I' as a single persona. Although he discarded stanza I, he did use most of the lines from stanza II in the 1994 edition of *TBL* and, slightly altered, in this 1996 version:

The kind of suit a man of this age
must wear: single or double-breasted,
turn-ups – or not – on the trousers,
usual lapels; the right space between
the blue stripes of monogrammed shirts...

In both versions the lines are longer; the phrasing, changed to alter the rhythm, results in subtle differences in meaning. Many alterations between the 1994 and 1996 editions were linguistic changes: in word choice to ensure variety; in phrasing to avoid overlap and slackness; and in the tightening or re-ordering of the line to make it rhythmically stronger. What the poems from the first three books demonstrate in their different line-lengths and structure is that until O'Driscoll scribbled that first eleven-line stanza at the check-out counter of the supermarket, he had not yet found the stanza form he needed to sustain a long treatment of his subject – to make poetry about work, work. With the structure established, he now needed the language to animate it. For O'Driscoll, "Poetry is loyalty to language before it is a loyalty to anything else".

Barbara Brown

The language and the rhythms of the language in *TBL* record authentic experience. O'Driscoll was drawing upon actual occurrences in a particular job he held in Dublin Castle where he was directly involved in statutory matters, company reorganisation and amalgamation, and was dealing with financial controllers and corporate lawyers. O'Driscoll: "We spoke a creative language, with new words being invented and abandoned all the time" (Kate Donovan, *Irish Times*, 22 January 2000). He used this language to create the poem's milieu and persona-narrators.

Over 200 examples of colloquial phrases, clichés, jargon, or slang, form the basic skeleton and unite the 550 lines of the poem. Examples of jargon are primarily associated with the business world: "clinch a deal", "hands-on management", "questions from the floor", "spread sheets", "debenture stock", "downward phase", "economic cycle". Numerous clichés, although directly associated with the office are not necessarily derived from it, such as "a meaningful existence", "sure of my own ground", "sweat of the brow", "dog-eat-dog mentality", "the same rut", "in my prime", "destined for the top", "scale the heights", "weak links". Many of these hackneyed phrases could be applied outside an office context, but *TBL* places them firmly within its domain. Fourteen examples appear in stanza 49:

> Some *networking* is necessary to *get*
> *To the right people, turning on the charm*
> Having them *eat out of your palm*, but never
> put entirely *on the spot, everything off*
> *the record*, a *once-only concession* you
> won't mention to your friends, *strictly*
> between yourselves, *without prejudice...*
>
> Futile dealing with less senior staff,
> *Sticklers for detail, holding progress back.*
> At clubs, committees, conferences, *make a point*
> *of banging heads together, picking brains.*

In stanza 50, examples in the last three lines include jargon and the climactic cliché – "the bottom line":

> At the end of the day, for my successors too,

> what will cost sleep are market forces, vagaries
> of share prices, p/e ratio, *the bottom line*.

Normally a poet seeks the unexpected, the fresh way of saying; metaphor revitalises the language, even as clichés denote tired, over-used metaphors. What makes this poem different is that its apparently casual, even 'lazy', use of everyday language is incorporated into the imaginative life of the poem, and thereby given renewed energy. By placing trite, worn-out metaphors within the poetic form, O'Driscoll achieves an act of reinvigoration.

Episodic vignettes focus on the professional and private experiences of the poem's persona-narrators. O'Driscoll explains: "Each stanza was an attempt to represent a state of consciousness or mind which I recognised as being true either from my own experience or experiences I had observed or could empathise with in some way" (*Cobweb*, 30). All kinds of inconsistency are apparent in the speakers: some are likeable, some not; some sympathetic, others are not; a few are self-assured, arrogant, others are wary, pressured, many are depressed, and a few are optimistic. The development is not of character but of theme.

For example: in stanza 1 the first speaker projects the anxiety and frustration permeating his bureaucratic world:

> Official standards, building regulations,
> fair procedures for dismissing errant staff:
> my brain is crammed with transient knowledge
> – patent numbers, EC directives, laws.
>   ...
> I race the engine, inch the car towards the green.

Another voice is despondent, numbed by the tedium:

> Scarcely to be acknowledged even to myself,
> days when the very sight of my wall planner
> makes me sick, when – instead of tough,
> decisive judgements, delivered with a quick
> peremptory scrawl – I sculpt a paper clip... [37]

Barbara Brown

Younger, more optimistic speakers describe: "Quality time at weekends, domestic bliss" and "...you feel your life has turned/up trumps and there are always/further heights to aim for".

In the familiar terminology of the job, another expresses his determination, perhaps desperation, to succeed:

> Not afraid of risks, not listening to
> cagey advice; striking out from time
> to time, irrespective of whose toes
> you're forced to tread on – whatever's
> needed to bring your plans on-stream.
> ...meanwhile, stand your ground. [46]

Some communicate the futility of their lives: "The hidden pain of offices", "profitless minutes", 'the shredded waste of hours', coupled with the "Anxieties you could elevate/to the level of mid-life crisis":

> Here I am
> in the same rut, not a single resolution
> carried through, deluding myself that
> I'm still in my prime... [26]

> Who will remember my achievements when
> age censors me from headed notepaper? [50]

After writing 'SELF-PORTRAITS', O'Driscoll completed the fifty stanzas of *TBL* in a particularly intense and productive two-month period. "I thought it would go on forever", he now says, speaking of what has been called the 'enabling power' to transmute the mundane into something more permanent. Why fifty stanzas? O'Driscoll is not sure, he cannot answer that question now. A symbolic reference to a middle-aged figure? A mid-life audit, balance sheet? A mystical number? (50 X 11 = 550? Beowulf's fifty year reign and the Dragon's length?)

As the poem was finished, he did a job swap to Customs; ironically by its 1994 publication he was Assistant Principal in International Customs in the office at Dublin's South Great George's Street, where he presently works. O'Driscoll says:

"It was an extraordinary coincidence that it became an elegy for the job that I held. Ever since I was sixteen years of age I was in the one area of work in Dublin Castle, that's twenty-eight, thirty, years? I thought I was going to go on until I was sixty-five" (*Cobweb*, 31). The language of *TBL* is no longer that of his current day job.

For O'Driscoll *TBL* also marks a major shift in style from the visual to the aural. As a young poet, O'Driscoll specialised in short, tight, image-driven poems. But *TBL* contains some effective images, which evoke its environment. Among many, one example:

> When you unclasp your slimline briefcase,
> the apple, deep green, high gloss
> with waxen sheen, a tea-break snack,
> glows among the acetate reports,
> symbolising something you can't name
> but crave for...

Otherwise enthusiastic reviewers have regretted the poem's sense of fatalism, found it depressing in its bleakness, and have accused O'Driscoll of not including the affirmative qualities which prompted him to care enough to re-create it, to redeem office life. But these critics seem to have missed the wistful voice within the poem itself, which acknowledges the yearning for something – "something you can't name but crave for" – beyond the materialistic:

> A Sunday walk: bees nuzzling perennials
> something stirring under roadside furze... [45]

or

> ...who can tell, later than you may rise
> to a weekend cottage, hens, a bright-red door... [8]

If such powerful images do not describe a redemptive moment, they evidence recognition of the need for redemption.

O'Driscoll admits to being fatalistic, but argues that his fatalism combines both pessimism and optimism. He believes in the catharsis of poetry: that in the act of putting down negative aspects of a problem – or a cultural phenomenon – one has begun to solve the problem. If for the reader the poem is totally depressing, it is a failure as a work of art. The following stanza from *TBL*, he cites as, "the truest stanza for me I've ever written":

> Then the time comes when you know
> none of your promise will be fulfilled;
> the saving roles luck, fame, deliverance
> from your job were meant to play...
> You will slave until pension day,
> eluded by advancement, satisfaction, wealth.
> In your head, some plangent melody repeats;
> in your mind's eye, a preview of your part
> as a walk-on stoic, accepting failure in good
> heart, battling home against the wind
> this night the same as last. [28]

Quality Time and O'Driscoll's fifth volume, *Weather Permitting*, contain poems which reflect an overflow of the subject matter and qualities of *TBL*, although not its stanza form. When O'Driscoll was preparing the new poems for *Quality Time*, at least two – 'Talking Shop' and 'Success Story' – echo the voices of *TBL*. The speaker in 'Success Story' also addresses himself in the second person: "You have turned the company around /...At the height of your abilities":

> To your astonishment, the question
> Of an early severance package comes
> Delicately over coffee, low-key
> "Can you pass the sugar, please?"

'Talking Shop' focuses on the small businessman who owns a neighbourhood grocery store, and who works seven days a week:

> What does it profit a man to own the pokey
> grocery store he sleeps above, unlocking at eight,
> not stopping until some staggeringly late hour?

The wry usage of the verb 'profit' with its relationship to the noun 'prophet', sees the prophet in the 20th century brought to mere profit. If rewritten in the eleven-line stanza form, both poems, but in particular 'Success Story', might have beenincorporated into *TBL*. Three poems in *Weather Permitting*, – 'The Celtic Tiger', '9 a.m.', and 'Delegates' – moving from narrow to broader views of commercial life, again draw upon a variety of poetic structures. What is new in these later poems is a sense of O'Driscoll's confidence after completing *TBL*, in his ability to make fresh use of stale contemporary language and to let the disembodied voice of the poem speak without supporting commentary.

A detached chronicler, O'Driscoll offers us a witty, humane verse, memorialising the 'wasteland' of the business office and boardroom. The tone is often ironic, but never satiric, objective yet sympathetic. Thematically, O'Driscoll depicts the dispiriting bleakness and soul-destroying isolation of the life of millions of people today, but also its possibilities of redemption. Here the jargon and clichés of the world of work of the late 20th century are perpetuated in their living form, transformed by the power of language. The integrity of the poem derives in large part from this ephemeral and non-standard language "really used by men", in Wordsworth's famous dictum. In *The Bottom Line* O'Driscoll has given us not only an unprecedented subject for Irish poetry but also a lucid commentary on that subject, timely and valuable. Today, his is a voice that needs to be heard.

Quarrying the Acreage of the Imagination
Matthew Geden interviews **Desmond O'Grady**
Kinsale, June 2000

Desmond O'Grady was born in Limerick in 1935. He left Ireland in the 1950s to begin a life devoted to poetry and travel. Since then he has lived in France, Italy, Greece, Egypt and America, returning in recent years to his home in Kinsale. O'Grady has published numerous books of his own poems as well as translations and versions from many different languages including, most recently, the *Selected Poems of C.P. Cavafy*. He is currently working on a long-term project, *The Wandering Celt*, which is a reflection of his own identity against the backdrop of the development of Western civilisation.

How do you approach the writing of a poem?

I'm inclined to think in terms of themes and so, in my daily life, I'm more aware of all the new daily revelations, the things that touch me. We all experience these all the time, some are stronger than others. When I'm working on a particular theme I'm much more conscious of how I see it reflected in life around me, in nature and in human nature or from my own memory. I use immediate experience and the experience of memory, I also connect personal thoughts with things I've read in a book – an epiphany of connection.

I write down notes, maybe an expression that comes to mind, perhaps something modern day. The important thing is to start something on the page, to write something down. The theme might be memory, it might be living in a small place like Kinsale, thinking of someone I knew forty or fifty years ago in faraway Rome. It might be about the first ghettos which were created in the area of Rome where I lived. There is a poem in the origin of the word 'ghetto', just as there is in the word 'Kinsale' or the word 'Ireland'. I tend to look for links in the etymological origins of the words.

Do you have a regular writing day?

Yes, I have a regular writing day and have had ever since I was in boarding-school when I fitted writing into my study hours. I used to devote an hour to working on a poem for myself, the other hours were for study, class and other activities like playing rugby. Writing a poem is a bit like playing rugby. You throw the ball around and every ball you throw is a word. So, you have to juggle the ball and each time you see it, it's a different word and there is a poem in that process as well.

Your work draws heavily on Western culture and the history of it.

Well, my most recent work does. The obvious beginning of that is 'The Dying Gaul' which was inspired by a statue that was made by the Greeks, discovered in Turkey, copied by the Romans and seen by me in Rome. It inspired a whole book of poems, I didn't know at the time that Byron had also written a poem about it.

Living in Rome I had to quarry everything that was around me and slowly learn, so I travelled to Greece, Egypt and also to America. It was all very different to Patrick Kavanagh, for example, quarrying from half an acre in Co. Monaghan. The half acre is ultimately the imagination. I don't know how many acres there are in the imagination, but in the acreage of the imagination one must quarry, or pasture.

Would you say that the modern experience of life can be illuminated by the ancient experience of life?

Of course. When one reads today about John F. Kennedy's young son being killed in an aeroplane crash it reminds one of when he stood as a child saluting his father's coffin being taken to burial. It might also remind someone else, like me, of Caesar's son by Cleopatra who was murdered in Roman times. On another level, the last thing Caesar said was, "And you too, my child" because there was a rumour that Brutus might also have been his child. Cavafy could have made a lovely poem out of that, but that's a question about finding one's personal voice in poetry. We poets all have to find our own voice as does someone writing prose. Some people find a steady one, for others it changes. They may start out with a lyric voice, but that voice may break as what one wants to say changes too. Ezra Pound's last poems, for example, were all very lyric. After the heavy, epic and dramatic dogmatism of *The Cantos*, he returned to the lyric of his early youth.

Matthew Geden

Rome seems to play a pivotal role in your work; the experience of Rome, Rome as a city and as a centre of Western civilisation. Would you agree with that?

Yes, I do think Rome is the pivotal point. Paris was where, as a teenager, I longed to go to when I left Ireland, but I never wrote about Paris. I wrote a lot of love poems while I was there but nothing about the city. At eighteen or so I wasn't so history-conscious. However, when I went to Rome I was more conscious of it because it's a little more obvious. I was living in the Jewish ghetto which is just underneath the Capitol Hill and beside the Roman forum. Julius Caesar was murdered two blocks away. Furthermore, St Peter's was a few minutes walk away and so, slowly the presence of history at all its levels became more manifest as I became more settled and more aware. I began to see that I was Irish, a Celt, a Christian, now in Rome living a pagan life yet seeing the Pope everywhere. I worked in the Vatican library and broadcast on Vatican radio in English, so the question of history became reality and all the worry beads of awareness started to face together.

You stress personal experience and private relationships in your work a lot. Do you think that a poet's duty is first and foremost to himself and his own experiences?

Yes, you can only write about your own experiences. You can't write about the experience of others unless the experience of another is a reflection of one of your own. We are all human beings and have common experiences, but when it becomes more personalised then it becomes more immediately demanding as poetic material and as a possible poem.

You use, like Kavanagh, local characters and incidents in your work. What would you say to those who might accuse you of being parochial?

Well, they are absolutely right. People accused Kavanagh of being parochial, but he was above that. Patrick Kavanagh's greatness was in being able to see the totally human in the parochial and in that way he was no different from Dostoevsky or any of the other great nineteenth century Russian writers. There's no real difference between the state of mind of a farmer in Co. Monaghan and one in China. Yeats couldn't deal with all that and he hid behind his masks of formulaic mythology.

Would you see a connection between Kavanagh's work and your own?

Part of Kavanagh's greatness was that he schooled and educated himself and so his world is not my world although I do something similar with my world. So, I write a lot of reminiscence poems about friends or personal relationships because these are the figures, in the reality of my personal experience, who have affected me. There are many poems not written about people, but many of them are like statues in the museum of my personal life. We all have personal museums of our lives and in these are gardens with waterfalls, statues and pieces of sculpture. My work is inclined to be a walkabout in the museum and gardens of my personal experience. A garden may be a French garden, or an Irish garden using the natural and the wild. I read an essay on English and Irish gardens when I was at school and the differences affected me. I think my *Collected Poems* is a bit of a mixture of different types of gardens.

What are you working on at the moment?

As I said earlier, my travels have made me more and more conscious of history and brought me from 'The Dying Gaul' to a study of Celtic literature and language. I've been too scholasticised to be able to write like Kavanagh and a lot of my honest inspiration is muffled or even suffocated by scholastic curiosity, but everything has to have its echo or shadow. So, I finally got this idea of *The Wandering Celt* which reflects the Celtic sensibility wandering around Western culture and how that created my sensibility as it is today. I never read novels now, I read history instead. However, when I write about Caesar I don't write about him politically, I write about Caesar the man, living his private life. In many ways it's no different from Kavanagh going for a walk on his plot of land.

I've begun to look back more. I suppose that if I was a young man starting out now I might see myself as part of this American empire, but although I've travelled all over America I don't feel involved in that empire or any other. Nevertheless, somewhere in *The Wandering Celt* I have to get to the point where I confront Caesar/John F. Kennedy and there is a poem there that I've not yet written about the empire of my time when I was as young as Catullus. But, whereas Catullus is very critical of Caesar, I would not be so of Kennedy; although I might be of aspects of what produced him. By 'doing' you learn 'how' to do, by doing this long poem I'm learning how to do it. It echoes my historical awareness.

Do you see this particular poem as being ever-expanding because each time you reach a point there is always another point on the horizon?

Absolutely. I'm dealing with the Celt, the Semite and the Arab who came from three different areas of Eastern Europe. The Celts are a race associated with horses, the Semites with donkeys and the Arabs with camels. So, I have to write a poem about the horse, one about the ass and one about the camel. The ass carried Jesus into Jerusalem, a camel carried Mohammed to conquer Europe and the horse became the great image of man as conqueror. These are all distraction poems. I'm trying not to be dogmatic, I'm trying to remain human and at the same time to reflect an awareness of culture which might be of interest to someone else's awareness and curiosity. In that sense there is always a schoolteacher in me, although I'm not trying to lecture anyone.

In *A Portrait of the Artist as a Young Man,* Joyce said, "Go forth and encounter the reality of experience" and that is what I did in love, marriage, children, happiness and also despair, poverty, unhappiness. Now, I finally discover I'm back to being a monk again, even a hermit. Yet, within my hermitage I have an entire world created by myself. I've lived many full lives and what I've tried to scribble down is my record of that and hopefully the record will be remembered by our grandchildren.

Is it important for you to leave a record?

I want to leave a memory or a contribution to the next generation. I'm no missionary, it's really for myself so that at the end I've exhausted all my human experience and am ready for the next life, if there is one.

I suppose that poetry itself is continuously expanding because new interpretations are brought to light on, for example, Kavanagh and Yeats, and this enriches their work.

You begin to see life more richly. When I was first reading Kavanagh the critics were all laughing at him, including my school friends, but I thought he was superb even though I had no experience of the countryside at all. I never went out there, but Kavanagh had his kingdom and it was a kingdom of the imagination which is more long-living than one of terra firma. So I treated Kavanagh as a prince when he came to see me in Rome. I brought him round and introduced him to all the other princes of European literature as a prince and he loved that.

It seems to me that you are ahead of many Irish poets in that you have a European perspective and have had that perspective a long time before any of your contemporaries.

Thank you and maybe, but what do I do about the American empire or the Chinese empire? The difference between East and West is very great, while the influence of Arabic on the European is fundamental. We wouldn't have Dante, Shakespeare and Petrarch without the Arabs, as I hope my book *Trawling Tradition* shows. In one sense those translations fit into *The Wandering Celt*. Anyway the first poem in my new book is a love poem, a translation from the Sumerian. It is the first love poem that we have in writing in the Western hemisphere. It's a short marriage piece written from the female perspective around 2000 BC give or take a year or two. So, I start with that and hopefully before I die I'll end with a love poem as well.

Desmond O'Grady

Siren

She surfaced here by chance. She'll dance all night
among we boys and girls as if on wing
with love. By day, her stroll the village street
brings song to old men's minds, smiles to the young.

Statuesque her carriage. Obsidian black hair
falls down her shoulders like unrolled manuscripts.
Gracious her face. Balanced her features there.
Those eyes reflect love's oriental markets.

Her icon nose ascends from mounted cheekbones
flanked by seashell ears, kissed, whisper back.
Her lips the sides of a half-open book of poems
will tell the pages' contents should she speak.

That tabernacle of her mouth contains
the sacred mystery of love's secret smile.
The column of her neck stands pure Dorian
on sculpted scapula mount her cupola breast-hill.

Her stroll's a glimpse of some Grecian statue
that moves and gives when her sanctuaries close.
A man would live his three lives out in virtue
of the hope that her sanctuary's all his.

All I behold smiles in her eyes were mine
a while and sirened me through my life's sail.
Now they sing out to my lone heart again
and swing my sail's gybe for that shore, her soul.

Desmond O'Grady

Hugh O'Neill in Rome
29 April 1608 – 20 July 1616

Exile chosen, they got here. That pursetight
Pope Paul V housed them without beds or furniture
on a common soldier's miserly monthly pay.
They survive on this Papal-Spanish pension.
We praise their frugal daily life, his fortitude
in his Irish cause nine years here among us.

He's the man who invented Ireland's guerrilla
war on England with the success of a Castro.
He won, but lost. Now he must face the facts:
He'll die in exile, with plans to invade Ireland
with troops from Spain to create his own Irish
Catholic nation protected by the Spanish navy.

His first restless years in Baroque boomtown
Rome he saw his forced stay as brief, before
return and conquest. Meanwhile, back home family
and friends have been executed by England;
in Rome they die of fever. That makes him one
of us émigrés who live around the eternal city.
He does not live our Rome's indulgent lifestyle.
His spirit's not broken. He's focused, courageous.
After daily Mass he sits to enormous
correspondence with Spain, Flanders, Ireland,
his stingy Pope to plead his cause and needs.
For exercise he climbs that gardened hill to

the Spaniard's church in Montorio. Raphael's
Transfiguration hangs over, Beatrice Cenci's
corpse lies under the high altar. Outside,
his view of Rome's ruins and winehills necklace.
A spectacle that's the heart of the Catholic world.
His heir lies buried here aged twenty-three.

Desmond O'Grady

Spanish-English peace pacts thwart his high hopes
for Ireland. Some say this daughter by his fourth wife
Catherine wastes their money on young girls' follies.
At night some wine conjures his past great years
while darkness lengthens, indifferent to his estate.
Tomorrow won't change human nature, or his.

He sees now what then failed: his peasants' frailty
and the strength of those forces he couldn't control.
Ambition galvanised him yet he recoiled
from that. His type of tragic hero is driven
by reason's inflexible demands which nature
denies. He epitomises his country's defeat.

For him the Counter Reformation gave the world
independence and self-development.
That is modern. Eurovision. That way
the Gaelic world could last. He hopes the Irish
see this and will unite in warwork for it.
If they all fail, it's merely human failure.

The future Ireland he would build would take
its independent place in our new Europe.
As the first Renaissance Irishman he's no
insular patriot self-exiled in dour defeat.
He still lives on as an Irish Euro with vision
and begs to be sent home with troops to conquer.

Self-insight in such men crowns or crucifies.
The comedy or tragedy of human acuity masks each
monarch or martyr. Ireland's atavism martyred him.
Does solace in his European ideals comfort him?
No, his pride affirms. At night his tiger's
eyes stare at those flambeaux in his wineglass.

All clip the Irish drunkards. It's said he takes
his rouse and drains his draughts...which takes from his
achievements the pith and marrow of his attribute...
One saw him tide and ebb his glass and taunt
his beard till his huge frame shook with sour sobs
and slumped across the table. Wine spilled like blood.
Thirty years he workwarred hard to mature
his world. He failed. O'Donnell died six years past
in Spain; their victor Queen Elizabeth I
(God is my oath) thirteen years gone, at seventy.
They say he takes his naked sword to bed.
Rumoured sick he may not last this summer.

Finis

When Spain advised against, would not finance
his wife's return to Flanders for health reasons,
O'Neill withdrew after New Year's to private life.
Unwell, they bled his legs an ounce a day two weeks.
Shakespeare died, sudden, April. O'Neill in July.
Would that the former wrote a tragedy on the latter.

With church pomp and solemnity O'Neill
was buried in San Pietro in Montorio
beside his son. Spain paid the funeral costs.
His sword hangs in St. Isidoro's. His wife
got his pension, moved to Naples, died there.
If here 1600, would O'Neill burn Bruno at the stake?

Roma, 30 December 1999
Roma, 6 February 2000

The Words We Use: A Look at the Poetic Voice

Bernard O'Donoghue

I think for a poet the struggle from the beginning is to really find the confidence and authority of your own voice, not only in terms of style but how to get to the point where what you're writing on the page is, metrically and in terms of tone, the exact voice in which you speak.

Derek Walcott

Observations such as this about 'voice' have become very common in the discussion of writing, of poetry in particular; indeed the term 'voice', which only began to be used as a critical term in the twentieth century, has become indispensable. But deciding on the literal meaning of the term presents the same kind of problems as Wordsworth's ideal of writing in the language "really used by men". As everyone notices, Wordsworth's poetic practice drew on very different vocabulary from what is used in everyday, ordinary language. In *The Prelude* he uses words such as "diurnal", and declared his poetic programme in these elevated terms: "for with my best conjecture I would trace Our Being's earthly progress". Wordsworth can't really be suggesting that this is the language of ordinary speech, so what does he mean? And what can Walcott mean by advocating that what the poet writes on the page must be the exact voice in which "you speak...metrically and in terms of tone"? Tone is a vague term, but people don't speak metrically in the poetic sense; surely the poet can't literally write in their own 'exact voice'?

And yet most writers and critics would assent to the truth of what Walcott says, in some sense. When a new writer is praised for having 'their own voice' from the start, as Seamus Heaney was in *Death of a Naturalist* in 1966, we feel we know what is meant. It connects to other terms like 'style', 'accent' and 'note'. It is striking too that this notion of individual voice has been particularly influential in the discussion of Irish poetry – maybe only Irish poetry in English. Commentators on such Irish poetry in the nineteenth century often used the phrase, 'the Irish note', a phrase that became linked with an odd and exclusive phrase, 'racy of the soil'. But beyond the local and dialectal associations of these terms, 'voice' claims an affinity with the particular writer's personal speech, suggesting that we would recognize not only a particular writer's place of origin and the kind of general poetic language that they write in, but also their individual practice within that wider linguistic community.

Of course in arguing for the "authority of your own voice", Walcott is warning against the practice of learnt poetic diction: the assumption of a distinct voice – a 'poetic' one – for writing poetry, which has no connection with the writer's normal speech. In the same spirit as Walcott's, over the past few decades many Irish poets – Heaney and Tom Paulin for example – have turned for their ideal of poetic language to the early nineteenth-century English Romantic poet John Clare. Clare was born of farm-labouring stock in rural Northamptonshire, and what Heaney and Paulin both admire is his fidelity to the language of that area. In an essay in *The Redress of Poetry*, 'John Clare's Prog', Heaney praises Clare for using the word 'prog', rather than the standard English word 'poke' or 'prod' in his mouse poem:

> I found a ball of grass among the hay
> And progged it as I passed and went away.

Heaney contrasts Clare's practice with his own failure to stay with the local term 'wrought' in his much-loved early poem 'Follower', which originally began:

> My father wrought with a horse-plough,

using the local Co. Derry verb for farm working. But in the published version of the poem in *Death of a Naturalist*, as well as in the three editions of *Selected Poems* published over the years, the line appears as:

> My father worked with a horse-plough,

substituting the Standard English verb 'worked', and thus, Heaney says in the Clare essay, losing "the one touch of individuality that had appeared in the first version".

So why, we might ask, did Heaney not restore the word 'wrought' in his authoritative large Selected Poems *Opened Ground* in 1998, if this is really the poem's element of true individuality? What Heaney knows, of course, is that the matter is a good deal more complicated than this. 'Wrought' may be the local dialect word, but that does not necessarily mean that it is the word which best corresponds to what Walcott calls the poet's "own voice... in terms of tone". Faithful as he is in all ways to his Derry origins, Heaney's practice – like Wordsworth's – is more than phonetic or lexical reproducing of the language of his locality. As soon as an expression is translated into poetry, it moves away from – maybe beyond – the

Bernard O'Donoghue

local. But it must not move outside the poet's own voice, however hard to define that idea is. In fact Paulin offers an enlightening opposite case: even though he has a strong Northern Irish accent himself, the elements of Ulster language he uses in his poetry are not part of his own spoken dialect: 'sheugh', 'yella', 'real good', 'a brave long while', and so on. The language they belong to is Paulin's chosen poetic voice, which is closely based on the dialect of Northern Ireland.

Paulin praises Clare for writing a language that can be socially opposed to the deadening Standard language, and we can see that the poetic voice he is assuming himself is consistent with this. But the case of Heaney's 'wrought' is rather different, one which goes further towards explaining why Heaney – like Wordsworth – cannot confine himself to the local term. If Heaney had published 'Follower' in 1966 with the original line, it would have been clear to a Co. Derry reader why he used the word. But it would not have been clear to the wider readership that publication by Faber in London aimed at (and it is rare for newly published poems to have explanatory notes attached). The word 'wrought' would not only have been obscure; it would have had an air of poeticism to it because to the world of English poetry (as distinct from the spoken language) it belongs to the tradition of poetic diction, as in 'a well-wrought urn': the last thing Heaney would want in this lucid, local poem. Far from expressing the local, it might have suggested an elite language reserved for poetry. The truth is that no language in the world of canonical literature is so difficult to achieve as a local usage that carries over naturally into the general language. It is, to use Heaney's term about Patrick Kavanagh, a 'chancy' business. Both the title and the opening lines of Kavanagh's poem, 'Kerr's Ass' are risky, exhilaratingly faithful as they are to Kavanagh's native Monaghan dialect:

> I borrowed the loan of Kerr's big ass
> To go to Dundalk with butter.

The poem survives the risk and ends magnificently with the "god of imagination" walking "in a Mucker fog". It is an exemplary case of successful representation of Walcott's principle. But even here it might be asked how precisely the cosmopolitan readership of poetry responds to the tone of this. Like the Derry reader's grasp of Heaney's 'wrought', a reader familiar with the tautological construction 'borrowed the loan' will take it in their stride better than the reader to whom it is unfamiliar.

The conclusion then is maybe that Walcott's statement, like Wordsworth's, is an abstract ideal. Except when you are speaking out loud, 'your own voice' is an abstraction. As far as poetry is concerned, the oral tradition does genuinely employ the spoken voice; in poetry composed on the page the voice is a kind of background shadow (Yeats called metre "a ghostly voice" which particular instances of poetry have an indirect exchange with"). But Walcott is no less right for that, even in describing non-oral poetry; the writer has to recognize the voice they write in as their own, not something imitated from a tradition. This voice may in practice be a long way from local dialect, or it may be very near it; it may be a perfectly standard usage, or it may be technically incorrect, like Kavanagh's "borrowed the loan". Kavanagh's lines are no more his own voice than this piece of relaxed standard language is in Heaney's:

> The annals say: when the monks of Clonmacnoise
> were all at prayers inside the oratory,
> a ship appeared above them in the air.

This is just as much at ease with itself as Kavanagh's practice; what Walcott is saying is that you have to be as confident with your poetic voice as with your normal speech. And it is easy to think of examples, in good songs especially, of poetry which belongs to the spoken and written tradition equally, as in Bryan MacMahon's verse in 'The Valley of Knockanure':

> The summer sun is setting now behind the Feale and Lea.
> The pale, pale moon is rising high way out beyond Tralee.

The quality of all these examples, I suppose, is naturalness: the naturalness that confers the confidence and authority that Walcott wants. I have given Irish examples, but Walcott's own poem 'The Schooner Flight' is a perfect example too. His West Indian voice is balanced perfectly between the reassured ease of the local and the universally intelligible. As with all matters of aesthetics, there are no absolute rules of right and wrong. As Walcott says, we have to find the voice in which we can say what we want to say in a way that sounds natural to ourselves and which doesn't sound as if we are affecting an accent; after all, if we don't believe in that voice, there is no chance that anyone else will.

Bernard O'Donoghue

Finnéigeas

Though failing in his lifetime quest for wisdom
when the boy burnt his finger on the salmon
and licked the pain, he got the better bargain
in the end. For, in his declining years,
it was his fireside that friends gathered by
to listen to the wisdom of his failures,
while know-all Finn, after whom were named
mountain-ranges and battlefields, was hated
by all for the miseries he caused and suffered,
and there was praise only for the man who'd killed him.
And ultimately Finn's wisdom told him this:
no one loves a wise man, not even himself.

Bernard O'Donoghue

The Quiet Man

One of the great films, by universal consent,
It could have been called 'The Quiet American',
Or, for that matter, 'The Violent Irishman':
Trim John Wayne, not easily roused, but once roused
His vengeance a wonder to the western world,
With Maureen O'Hara, for all her wish
For independence, kicking impotently
On his shoulder. We saw it in Manchester,
The year of the Korean War, when films ran
Continuously. We came in, aptly enough,
At the culminating meadow fight,
Stayed for Tom and Jerry and the Pathé News,
Before leaving at the point we'd started at,
With McLaglan lying battered in the hay.

Introduction to the winners of our Poetry Competition
Bernard O'Donoghue

As in the previous two years, the competition attracted a large number of entries (even more than previously) with a wide range of skills and interest. The autobiographical-rural has made a big comeback, and it is a form in which there is great competence now. There was a lot of penetrating irony, especially by women writers. Anne Dean's 'Mirrors are Funny' combined the reminiscence and social setting with great subtlety; Mary O'Gorman's 'Chicago, Chicago' did it with her customary wit and edge. Nigel McLoughlin's 'Subjects' was unusual (and outstanding) in having objectivity and a steady eye and hand; music and drawing coalesce in the unforgettable production of the image, suggesting the fascinated intrusion of art with great tact and delicacy. But I ended up liking Tommy Curran's poems best of all this year, by a short head. "Those two men in a van/stopped near the lights/on Pope's Quay" images perfectly the everyday as you "empty yourself into the city". It is the same quiet and unjudging observation of the social scene that is pleased to watch the streets filled "with shoppers, in from the mountains/and the sea" ('Of a Christmas Eve'). This is an immensely likeable new voice, a distillation of the observant and humane qualities that seem to me to characterise the best entries for this competition every year.

First:	*In February, In for the Day*	**Tommy Curran**
Second:	*Subjects*	**Nigel McLoughlin**
Third:	*Mirrors are Funny*	**Anne Dean**

In February, In for the Day

Seen at this narrow angle
and in the channel
of its limestone walls
the river flowing fast
from under Northgate bridge
the way the dark water catches your eye!

The way the light is diffuse and the air
is cold and squally. The way you sit here
thinking "on higher ground it must be snowing
north-west Cork probably...
be blowing into drifts whiter
than the white coats of the mountain sheep".

and those two men in a van
stopped near the lights
on Pope's Quay, the way their anonymity
overflows them, filling your need
to be anonymous as the Lee
at Roche's Point.

The way, waiting in traffic
on Shandon Street hill
you are going with the non-flow
but all the while
emptying yourself
into the city.

Subjects

I
He's keeping time with a pencil
on the page, to the slow air
the fiddler's bowing, drawing her.

He flicks the fine hair across her neck
shading her cheeks, her hands;
eyeing her, eyeing her constantly.

He's measuring her, all thumbs.
Angling her with pencils, stopping
sometimes, proportioning; divining her.

II
There is a feel of 3B about
her soft graphite eyes.
They never stray, remaining
fixed to the back wall, lost.

her hands are dancing, across
the fiddleneck, small hands
trimmed, with a scrubbed look;
feline in their fall across strings.

her face has a high colour
like an afterglow of blush,
perhaps from the effort of playing,
perhaps aware she's being sketched.

Mirrors are Funny

I'm sitting in the rocking chair
opening and shutting
mother's compact.
Father is behind me
and I can tell from the sound
he is shaving again.

I hold up the compact
and see his face
in his shaving mirror. His skin
is stretched across his jaw,
his razor carving a path
through foam covered shadow.

Mother leans over me,
her face in the mirror
she checks her skin,
smiles at me and moves away,
soaks up blood
from a nick on father's chin.

He bleeds easily.
I look at my face
and move the mirror
down the knitted cable
on my jumper,
and my new kilt,

examine bruises on my knees,
first the one, then the other,
and my white socks.
And my new brown shoes.
The mirror can hold all of us,
separately. I find myself, seeing me.

Tommy Curran

Of a Christmas Eve

In Cork this morning all is Pagan!
Last night we took it in turns
going out to the off-licence for more
and more wine to fuel our raucous singing.
And afterwards, over strong coffee,
we just talked; stories in the early hours,
a quietening down...of when souls came
up into mouths like earthworms,
from deep in soil, crawl out into warm rain.
We said how love's changed us.

In Cork this morning, under an opaque sky,
many gulls are in on the Lee (in full tide)
and all the streets are filled
with shoppers...in from the mountains
and the sea.

A Bucket of Fresh Water

Half a hundred years ago, anchored north of the point
in a busy-as-Grand Central bed of weeds
beside the drop-off into darkness,
I stare down, feelin' privy to another world,
watch, wait, pay out a foot or tow of line,
snag him, enjoy the bit of fight,
unhook perch, one skittery fella after another,
suckers for dangled worms, drop 'em
into a bucket of regularly renewed water,
watch 'em swim about between bare feet,
non-stop turnin'.
They stay that extra bit fresh.

After making the rowboat safe,
transom fully two feet up from breakin' waves
I clean the catch right
before supper
on a piece of flat driftwood
at the edge
of the lake,
flick the guts to gulls.
And Gramma fries the little fellas up,
once in a while a bass.

Now I do much the same
with dreams:
when I'm first aware
of bein' awake,
when I spot 'em dartin' off,
I hook 'em,
put 'em in a bucket of fresh water,
watch 'em turn & turn about,
make nothin' of 'em,
just keep 'em nice
'n fresh
until it's time for breakfast.

Dympna Dreyer

Redundant
after G. Holloway

You hoarded, all our married life.
"Waste not, want not, my father said!"
You loved old things but not your wife.

A sugán handle, a thatcher's knife,
a large portrait of Uncle Ned,
you hoarded, all our married life.

It was a source of constant strife.
"Their place is in the garden shed!"
You loved old things but not your wife.

A mouth organ, a battered fife;
"I once was musical," you said.
You hoarded, all our married life.

"New things cost a bomb!" you chide,
then settled for a brand new bed.
You loved old things but not your wife.

You cut from home clean as a knife
and left me nothing of yourself.
You loved old things but not your wife.
You hoarded, all our married life.

Mary O'Gorman

Chicago, Chicago

I remember walking to Mass
in my turquoise frock
swinging mother's hand
singing *I saw a man*
he danced with his wife
over and over and over again

"Stop that codology!" she snapped
glancing at father
a strange rage
in her eyes,
slim ankles shackled
in sturdy boots.

Anne Comerford

End of the Affair

She struggles to keep up
as their stroll
round the block
becomes a marathon,
his energy,
fuelled by anger,
dictates the pace
and soon
their walk
has become a race
and he is
beyond her reach

they come full circle
as the light dies

looking back
she remembers
how his curls
kissed his collar
as she ran behind.

Dark October

In the garden
on a dark October day
I pulled roped nasturtium stems
from a wooden tub.
Thumbed off ridged seeds
sat them in a shell
on the window sill.
Here they turned beige
for planting out in early June.

sown by the wall
warm thoughts of colour
in rich raked soil.

Through summer nasturtiums grew
spread to overflow.

Dimmed in red, orange, yellow
this October day.

Mary O'Donnell

Knight

As he sleeps, he reminds her of the tombs
of crusaders, full-scale stone effigies
that represent eternal rest for men

who rode south to fight the heathen.
The brows are dark and straight,
droop gently towards his temples, meet

the flickering incline of pale eyelids.
The nose is firm, mouth a closed line,
sealed against perfidy of thought or act,

the mind at rest while, round him, infidels prosper.
In dreams, he believes in miracles,
that good will vanquish the unquiet hour,

that serpents shrivel even as they enter
the houses of noble men, while unicorns
graze in his garden, lay pearly horns

in the lap of his lady; she sees him
there, in the weak dawn light,
before the first cars hum to life,

knows the honour of his sleeping time,
how she will never lie beside him on the tomb,
graven lady of silent mouth and rigid limb.

Joyce had Melon

Joyce had melon.
She must like it I suppose.
Anyway, she asked for melon.
I had soup.
As the plates were put before us
half a dozen sea-birds,
I don't know, some sort of sea-bird,
landed on the lawn
and started picking at the grass.
They came towards the window in a line
then turned
all together
like the limit of a wave
and worked back the other way.
Now and then we heard a marshy mellow whistle from them;
Strange to hear it there in town.
In fact the whole thing was strange;
my being there with Joyce,
blown so far off course;
the silent footsteps of the birds
teasing me,
not quite reminding me
of something willingly forgotten.
In the end I concentrated on the food,
the birds asked too much of my astonishment,
and before we finished eating
– both of us had trout,
very nice too –
I looked out and they were gone.
Not flown, I realised,
just unavailable among the trees.
as I was unavailable,
and as Joyce was too
across the table from me
thinking about cheese.

Nina Quigley

Summer Turns

Summer turns its face from her.
She grows thin, disconnects.
Soon, only the shy sting
of seagrass holds her.

She drifts out of radio contact,
lies for hours on her back
in the dunes,
eyes full of clouds.

She grows minimal,
universe reduced
to the jut of her knee,
a slice of bicycle wheel,
the play of wind
and peek-a-boo sun.

Beyond her vision,
the hot blue pulse
of the ocean withdraws.
She's orphaned
by the year's long heave
back from the centre.

Another Life: Michael Viney

in conversation with **Eugene O'Connell**

Michael Viney was born in 1933 in Brighton, England and left school at sixteen to join the local weekly newspaper as an indentured apprentice reporter. He worked later in Fleet Street, and joined *The Irish Times* in 1962 after 'a winter out' in Connemara. He became known for early investigative series on social problems and as a current affairs presenter on RTE, turning later to environmental issues. He married Ethna, a fellow journalist and RTE producer, in 1965 and their daughter Michele now works in media in Galway. The family moved to Mayo in 1977, when Viney began his weekly column 'Another Life' in *The Irish Times*. After two anthologies from the column, Blackstaff Press published his book *A Year's Turning* in 1996 (now republished by Penguin). Ethna Viney's book *Dancing to Different Tunes: Sexuality and its Misconceptions* was also published in 1996. Michael Viney was trained as an RTE producer-director shortly before his move west, and he and Ethna have made a number of documentary films and series for RTE and TG4. They are now working on a series of seasonal films based on *A Year's Turning*.

An appreciation of the environment is still a relatively new area of study in Ireland. What writers do you regard as pioneers in the field and how have they influenced you?

The writers who have had most impact with me have been people whose 'green' credentials arise from a personal and passionate celebration of nature. Rachel Carson for example, but as much for her trilogy *The Sea* – she was a marine biologist – as for *Silent Spring*, her 1962 polemic on pesticides which virtually launched the whole green movement. Or Barry Lopez, for *Arctic Dreams*, another superb environment book which scarcely mentions the word 'environment'. The witness of science-poets like these does a lasting job on what I'd loosely call one's soul.

Many of the writers who have shaped my ideas are American. A good starting point for any thinking about the human relationship with nature is the 'land ethic' set out by Aldo Leopold in his *Sand County Almanac* in 1949. His premise that our ethical interdependence with others should extend to soils and waters, plants and animals has been enormously influential. It helped set the scene for the modern 'deep ecology' movement founded in the 1980s on the ideas of Arne Naess, a Norwegian philosopher – ideas like respect for the intrinsic worth of all species, the need to limit human population to a sustainable minimum (100 million, I think, was Naess' figure), the need to be sure of what we're doing before we encroach further on environments and ecosystems. And this meshes of course with James Lovelock's thrilling metaphor of Gaia – the world as a self-sustaining, self-regulating organism.

'Deep ecology' is influencing a huge range of personal expression, from the daffiest of New Age lifestyles to really committed radicalisms like the protests at the World Trade Conference in Seattle and the tree-squatting at Glen of the Downs. By comparison, I'm very passive. I do my bit of 'thinking like a mountain' and talking to my plants. I've become rather misanthropic, and quite reject the idea that we have in any way a God-given right to exploit nature as we wish. That's on the emotional side. On the intellectual, I do deeply appreciate the scientific method of inquiry and the lack of anthropocentrism – ideally – in the presentation of results. I like the way James Lovelock insists that the idea of us 'harming' the planet is an extension of our sense of self-importance: if we get too far out of line, we shall be swept away and the next turn given to the ants.

Are you at all optimistic that we can reverse the seemingly inevitable consequence of global warming?

Not very: there's a lot of momentum in the process already, and more piling up behind in the industrial development and consumer expectations of China and the Third World. I think we are probably past the point where any technological fix can make up for the political inertia and resistance so far.

Was there a period in Earth's history that mirrored the disturbing events now being forecast?

Many thousands of them probably! Even within the natural climate cycles of the Earth, which depend very much on its orbit round the sun, there has been room for immense variation, even what we might see as chaos. The evolution of life itself has brought huge atmospheric change, held in equilibrium by the feedback mechanisms of the planet. But this is the first time, so far as we know, that the actions of a single species have had such impact on Earth's atmospheric chemistry and thus on climate.

What do you imagine will be the final consequence of global warming?

In Earth-wide terms, I have no idea. The melting of the polar ice-caps will raise sea level and flood low-lying coastal settlements, most destructively in the port cities of Dublin, Cork, Limerick and Galway. In our small corner of Europe, the critical factor could also be what this does to the patterns of ocean circulation. If, as seems possible, we lose the winter warmth of the Gulf Stream, we could end up with a climate as cold as Labrador's – plus hurricanes.

Are we pro-active enough in our efforts to reverse this trend?

Did you walk to work this morning?

Are you confident that the urgency of the situation is understood by the ordinary man in the street?

I think people have the general idea by now, but are not going to let it worry them – it's 'they', somewhere out there, who ought to do something about it.

What exactly does James Lovelock mean in his view of earth as 'a self-regulating superorganism'?

For the whole, very readable and exciting story, try his book *The Ages of Gaia* (1988). Briefly, his theory is that the Earth, its rocks, oceans, atmosphere and all living things, are part of one great organism evolving over the vast span of geological time. It uses elaborate feedback mechanisms to regulate the planet for the sustenance of life – all life that is, not just our own reckless and disruptive species. Gaia, the Greek earth goddess, is simply Lovelock's powerful metaphor.

What spiritual or religious implications do you believe Lovelock's theory has for humanity as a whole?

None, necessarily: it is the product of scientific inquiry and deduction. But the effort to appreciate the workings of ecology – the interconnectedness and interdependence of life – does engage a lot of the emotions that people recognise as spiritual. I'm sure you can believe in God and Gaia both, but it does leave the Judaeo-Christian conviction of man's superiority to, and apartness from, nature very much out in the cold.

How has your own experience of the alternative lifestyle affected your religious or spiritual views?

The sheer involvement with growing things, and with soil and weather, seems to have moved me on from agnosticism to a more positive Gaian paganism: I have, as it were, discovered my loyalties. At the same time, the more I learn of evolution at work, the more I have to come to terms with the element of chance in my own existence and survival. That can piss me off a bit, though of course it shouldn't.

Has your experience of 'Another Life' tempered the original romantic view you might have had of rural life?

I'm certainly a Romantic, it's the only thing worth being, but I don't think I ever had any fatal illusions about rural life. The biggest of them probably was that, once you could spend every waking hour in your own home, on your own bit of land, you could do all the things you've ever thought of doing. You can't – the days aren't long enough. So we never did get to go fishing in our currach, and I'm still not 'the well-known painter and sculptor'.

As for our early 'self-sufficiency' years, with goats, hens, bees, turf-cutting and the rest, we wouldn't have missed them for the world. We had very little money and worked incredibly hard from dawn to dusk, but the sense of independence was very satisfying. I once wrote in the column: "When you've got an acre of land and a house of your own, there's not much they can do to you." You certainly end up with a whole new perspective on money and security.

How were you received locally when you arrived first?

With great kindness and proper caution!

Was there a local tradition of conservation, say in the sayings or lore of the people?

There was, I think, a feeling that 'the old people' were better at co-operating to manage the use of the commonage; now, everyone's an individual, even the 'meitheal' for silage-making has gone. More than a decade ago, everyone could see the signs of overgrazing on the hills, but no one believed the community had any role in stopping it.

Have you detected a sympathy or tradition of conservation in our own native Gaelic culture redolent, say, of the great native American Indian tradition of love of the natural landscape?

Something like this does come through in Fergus Kelly's fascinating book, *Early Irish Farming* (1997), which examines the Irish law-texts of the seventh and eighth centuries. The motivation of these laws was certainly conservation and just use of resources; but whether this really linked in to the nature-lyricism of the early monastic poets – I have my doubts.

Is it fair to say that our historical experience of poverty has placed our concern for the environment lower down the scale of our priorities?

Yes, without a doubt. The historical dysfunction of colonial peasant culture, the ecological betrayal of the Famine, the identification of 'nature' with Ascendancy hobbyists, the dropping of Nature from the Free State school curriculum, the essential utilitarianism of farming – all these have helped breed the idea of 'the environment' as a dilettante, even alien, concern. Without the EU to set priorities and standards, I think we'd be a great deal further back. For some great insights into Irish attitudes to the earth sciences and nature, I'd recommend *Nature in Ireland: a Scientific and Cultural History* (Lilliput, 1997), a big fistful of essays edited by John Wilson Foster.

What writers or thinkers continue to move or inspire you?

More Americans – Edward O. Wilson (*The diversity of Life*), Stephen Jay Gould (any book of his essays), David Quammen (*The Song of the Dodo*). On evolution, any book by Richard Dawkins. At home, Tim Robinson (*Stones of Aran*) and sundry fine poets – Michael Longley and Eamon Grennan chief among them. For thinking, I prize provocative postcards from Gillies MacBain, organic sage and 'deep brown' philosopher, who writes from a tower in Tipperary.

Do you see yourself as part of the artistic community that seems to have traditionally congregated in the west of Ireland?

No. My move to the west was a personal challenge to engage with a more basic and balanced way of life. Writing was a bread-and-butter matter. As far as art is concerned, I haven't shown the dedication of the West's artistic community. I wish I'd been able to paint the west like Maurice MacGonigal did for the RHA, or like Sean McSweeney does now. But I still have hopes of putting oil painting first.

What sparked your own particular interest in line drawing, as distinct from water-colour or oil painting?

The need to illustrate my column each week and be paid for it!

Which artists, if any, have influenced your own style?

I particularly admire the black-and-white work of two very English masters: Samuel Palmer and Eric Ravilious.

Do you see any merit or relevance for the modern world in the Wordsworthian view of nature as 'Primal Teacher'? What in your opinion would be the proper way to look at nature in the light of recent developments like global warming?

I think Wordsworth would have got very excited about the insights of modern ecology. He would have been reassured in his intuitive response to nature as instructor and healer. John Stuart Mill, as an overstressed twenty year old, called Wordsworth's poems "a medicine for my state of mind", which is exactly what John Seed, with his deep-ecology "Council of All Beings", is trying to offer now. It's a pity that such sound emotion as Wordsworth's got so swamped by the gush of Victorian nature writing – but the daffodils are still going strong.

As to nature in the present environmental crisis, I want to ask: "Crisis for whom?" Nature will come out of this okay, minus perhaps the polar bears and a few other species that need ice in their world. Gaia will adjust to the new atmospheric regime, whatever this costs human economies and food supplies.

I was very moved and disturbed by an early book on global

warming, Bill McKibben's *The End of Nature* (1990). He made me realise what a loss it would be if we could no longer think of nature as wild and independent of us. A nature we have altered irredeemably seemed harder to love so much, or trust.

But now I see Gaia beginning perhaps to react to human impact, as new or resurgent viruses and extreme weather take a toll on populations. I don't mean at all to be callous, but why should our species be alone in escaping the usual and natural controls on population explosion?

You seem to have embraced technology, in contrast to some advocates of the more radical 'deep ecology'. Are you optimistic that we can accommodate technology and ecology for the benefit of both?

Technology is essential to finding ways of using and recycling materials and energy that are compatible with natural processes. We have to stop producing materials and waste products that are chemically synthetic and cannot be recycled. For a writer and filer-away of facts, the computer is seductive and now probably indispensable, but we shall have to start producing ones we can melt down again, or eat, and that don't use six buckets of oil to make. I do hanker a bit for the simple life we had in our early years here in Thallabawn – no car, no central heating and certainly not much money. But as one gets older, comfort corrupts.

The western seaboard has sometimes been seen as an alien or strange sort of other Ireland that was often seen as a bolthole for outcasts or misfits. What contemporary voices from the west do you regard as revealing or anticipatory?

People who run here, leaving some failure or disappointment, tend not to survive. We were making a deliberate choice about lifestyle, habitat and freedom to experiment. The western seaboard is as remote as you want or need it to be – it offers the same space and wind-music that nourished the monks on the Skelligs. I cherish voices that lift me up to new connections with nature – the meditations of Chet Raymo at Dingle, for example in his *Honey from Stone* (Brandon, 1997), or Tim Robinson's magical essays from Connemara. That neither is Irish is quite irrelevant: the west has been a mountain-top for the world.

Sheila O'Hagan

Stars are Charcoal

On this night
sky is a lake of moon-eyed fish,
stars are charcoal.

Distant and passionless
as a spire in winter
you take shape, then fade.

As though some bend in the road
might alter light,
I pull up, isolate

the space you seemed
to claim, stretch eyes
to pin you down.

Still you shadow me,
evade the intimate
as I drive home alone.

Dido and Aeneas

High on the poop deck sly Aeneas dozed
Dreaming of Troy and a favourable west wind
And as the dawn crept up he cast the ropes
That bound him to his Carthaginian queen.
Betrayed and shamed, poor Dido, from her tower
Made out the furl of his sails cut and run.
Across the water ran her screams: Aeneas, thief,

I salvaged you as flotsam on my shore.
Under the dripping stars you came and now
You sneak away by dawn's back door. I hate
Your Trojan towers, your father king.
I am a queen, not yours to cast aside
Before our marriage bed has lost its heat.
And so her scalding tongue ran on until

Her maids came running to console her.
But still she cried: He's left me without child
By whom to know him. Sisters, build a pyre,
Lay on it his clothes, all the sweet intimacies
He left by our bed. I loved them while the Fates
And God allowed. Leave me to watch them blaze.
When the women left, she climbed onto the pyre

And drew the sword she'd hidden in her robe
Then plunged down on it. But before she died
She drew across her face a veil of wild
Acanthus flowers Aeneas had given her
In their love throes. And from that bitter gift
A thousand gauzy stars rose up to pierce
The blackened sky above his scuttling ships.

Sheila O'Hagan

Mirage

When the boy appeared out there,
all wrapped in shimmering linen,
pale as the haze of noon,
his arms in flames, his eyes
full of his own being,

it was a visitation unheralded
that found me drowsy under
summer trees, the air so bright,
the boy so still, so shined,
wearing his ineffable peace.

Yet even as I fathomed him
his fading linen snooked
on the wind, the sun withdrew,
the earth shook itself and I
was left with rounded eyes

to shiver in the grass,
feel the waning day,
see the stilly hole
of light in the shaded tree
where a god has been.

Rainy Day In Annaghmakerrig

I

Strange how much of it, this rain
Flaying its way in needles and in sheets.
How clean the trees seem, how full of it

The lakes, and green the oh so greenish
Land beneath its laving. I see two cows
Against the hedge nudge each to each,

And a man out there, his head wedged hard,
his face abrasive. But I am inside,
My feet dry, looking out and gratified

As in cinema, to wade in dream
That goes on without me. Yet still
I feel, what can I say, rain, deprived?

II

Today if you can't get out, look out and see:
There is no wind, the lake can scarcely breathe.
(Those dark spires on the hill are evergreens).

Then try to hone your mood to be as still
And tune into the hum of misty rain
That spills onto the lake's old silver gleam.

Look there, a gloriously roundy copper beach
Assaults your eye with flare of after light.
As if you're out there, stop: within your reach

A grey fox, wraith-like, slinks across the lawn.
Now cows are moving up in two's and three's
To see who'll listen to their forlorn news.

Sheila O'Hagan

The lake, the grey, the green, the solitude,
The rinsing mist, the low flung muslin cloud
Seen from your window, set this day's late mood.

III

But should you go walking after rain
Look for left over wetness everywhere,
Rivulets on the paths, and light enough

Before twilight battens down what's left of day.
Watch for a swallow as she skims the fields.
And find the tree, untouchable, that holds

Her skirt ten feet above the ground. Maybe
A dragonfly will trail itself across the lake –
Wisp of fire; or a leaf drift over pebbles

Pocked with gold. Let your eyes linger
On what shines awhile, before all's shrouded
By the day's demise. Then listen to the night's long sighs.

My Working Life with Ted McNulty, A Memoir
Sheila O'Hagan

It seemed like a divine plot. Two born-again poets meet at a poets' paradise – the 1998 Yeats Summer School in Sligo. Ted McNulty had come from Baltimore, USA; I had come from London. Each of us had poems published in that quarter's issue of *Poetry Ireland Review*. There was an immediate bonding and a friendly one-upmanship. I was on page one, Ted McNulty was on page thirty-seven. The editor was the eminent poet, John Ennis, who became a valued friend.

At the end of the Summer School, I went back to London, and Ted to Baltimore in the US. The wrench of the parting initiated a flow of correspondence centred on poetry, and unequalled, I dare say, even by the Brownings. With such intensity plying the Atlantic, it was inevitable that we should meet up again. Both Ted and I had lost our partners – mine, sadly, through death; Ted, with equal sadness, through a failed marriage. But our relationship was not cemented through a common loss so much as a compulsion to write poetry.

I think that Ted's latent creative ability had been released by the death of his father, an Irish emigrant from Cavan who remained distant from Ted all his life. Ted's first poem 'Annointed' describes the experience, after the funeral, of sitting in his father's chair for the first time. It was more of a communion than a farewell, Ted said. "I lean back and I do it / I touch him at last." ('Annointed', *Rough Landings*, 1992)

My own 'flame' had been set alight in Dr Barbara Hardy's poetry workshop in Birkbeck College, London, where I was studying English Literature. Barbara, an inspiring tutor, started that great workshop while I was in my last year, laying it down that admittance depended on the production of some poems.

In 1989 Ted resigned his teaching post at Townson State University, Baltimore, to join me in London, where I had lived for thirty-five years. For a while we gave writing workshops in Wormwood Scrubbs, and went to 'The Blue-Nosed Café' in Islington to meet other poets. But Ted was uneasy in London. Together we made the decision to move to Ireland. In September 1990, we set up home outside Dublin, my native city, taking a flat in a Dalkey house with the lordly name of 'Prince Patrick'.

Sheila O'Hagan

In that cold-as-a-tomb Victorian mansion, our writing partnership started in earnest. We shared a study, amicably, from which we could see a handkerchief of sea. Round the corner was the splendid Vico Road, where we lived we could see right across Dublin Bay. At night the view was particularly spectacular with a serpentine necklace of lights round the black neck of the water.

Domestic life centred on the work desk. There was a reassurance in working alongside someone as deeply immersed in poetry as we both were, a trust, I suppose, in the shared purpose. All else in our lives was subservient to that ideal. Which is not to say we shut ourselves up like monks. Living near the centre of a writing world, we threw ourselves into the literary life of the city, through its many readings and launches.

For some three years, the Dublin Writers' Workshop was a meeting place. I was one of four facilitators, editing the poetry section of *Acorn*, its bi-annual magazine. We gave workshops in schools. I judged a writing competition for prisoners in Mountjoy, conducted on FM 98 radio. Both of us, in sequence, served as writer-in-residence for Kildare County Council, my term in 1995, Ted's in 1996.

In 1991, Ted had won the double Tribune Hennessy Awards for New Poet and New Writer of the Year. A journalist friend described him as "standing cuckoo-like among the young writers, chuckling at being new at fifty-six." It was a measure of his humility that, having been awarded the title of 'New Poet of the Year', he didn't hear the second announcement of his award for 'New Writer of the Year', and had to be pushed out of his seat to come forward and again receive the award from President Mary Robinson, as she then was.

Not to be outdone, two weeks later I won the Patrick Kavanagh Award for a first manuscript of poetry, and followed it in 1992 with the Tribune Hennessy. This pattern of being neck and neck, in recognition and in publication, was continued when in 1992 Ted's first collection, *Rough Landings*, and my first collection, *The Peacock's Eye*, were published by Salmon Poetry; in 1995, our second collections, Ted's *On The Block* and my, *The Troubled House*, were published by the short-lived Salmon/Poolbeg partnership.

In 1993, another move, this time to the centre of Dublin. We found an apartment in St Stephen's Green. Once more, we shared a workspace, in a large room on the third floor. From its three high windows, we stared straight into the magnificent trees of the Green. The noise of passing traffic below was like the rush of a distant river. It was almost pastoral. In this splendid location, our days were again organised around the need to write.

Working in a room with Ted, one would be aware of the intensity, the deep quiet he cast around him, the vast poetic meditation of the man. He turned his working space into a church. A nimbus of quiet and trance hung over his corner. I was calmed and, it could be said, blessed by that intensity. His desk seemed to me to be a clay bed that harboured the roots of memory, as if he were still looking for himself among the memories of his childhood. A friend remarked that "his best poems made you want to weep". I'd think Ted went into a trance when composing.

My own state was quite different, a sort of rhapsody, or to put it more prosaically, a mood of excitement or discovery. Ted was a one-session man. I suffered an addiction that might or might not end in a 'benediction'. The waste-bin was almost entirely filled by me. I worked fast on my old Amstrad. Once a poem started to reveal itself, I found the versatility of a computer very apt. The words could be arranged, the poem shaped directly on the screen. I could see how the poem was going to look. I didn't stay sacramentally still as Ted did. I moved around quietly, looking into books, notes, anything that might feed that unveiling. Once the thing was captured, I might work for weeks, maybe even months, on the editing, putting it away, taking it out again, waiting for the last right word.

Ted was very satisfied by the physicality of writing: when he used pencils, they were plain and sharpened; his pen would be a favourite, heavy in the hand so he was aware of it. He wrote on a lined A4 pad. His first draft would go down the left side of the margin; beside it on the right would be his corrections, his re-write. There might be several pages of re-writes, each beside the other, as far as possible. Ted, terrier-like, would hold onto his poem until the last beautifully-pencilled draft. When he was finally satisfied – and it could take days, in which he never really surfaced – he would type it out, two fingers flying over his much-loved typewriter. Then he would record the title in his book marked 'Ships in Dock', send it out with two or three others already recorded, and enter them into his book marked 'Ships at Sea'. A third book recorded acceptances. It was quite full.

Sheila O'Hagan

We occasionally wrote reviews. Ted's were excellent, replete with honesty and depth of perception. He didn't seize on the faults, as do some reviewers, hoping to make a name for themselves rather than promote the talents of the unlucky poet. Ted poked around the writer's soul until he put his finger on the particular vision in the work. His criticism was gentle but adamant. He never damned with faint praise but nor did he encourage mediocrity.

Working together as we did, it was inevitable that Ted and I looked to the other for the final imprimatur. And each of us gave due weight to the other's criticism. If it came to murdering our darlings, we were prepared to do so. I do think we helped each other greatly in this way. It drew us up and impelled that final 'think'. We acted as that audience out there, the reader waiting to be beguiled and convinced. But we never 'wrote' for each other. So different were we in our approach, our language, our listening, a poem would have collapsed had there been any obtrusive influence.

Ted, with his poetic honesty and concrete awareness, often tried to 'earth' me but I was sufficiently confident in my own style of expression to resist him. For my part, I don't think I ever tried to change Ted's mode of expression. I recognised the strength of its physicality, the imagination rooted in memory, and in direct accessible images. Medbh McGuckian, in her review of his collection, *On The Block*, spoke of "a self-consciousness ordering its experience rigorously and selectively, with economy and passion".

Although Ted was an enthusiastic reader of poetry, he was uninfluenced by other poets. His compulsion was to express himself as a loner, outside the camaraderie of the common man, his 'poetic' regret. That sense of isolation accounted for, I believe, his very individual voice. His emotions were rooted in a sense of unease with himself. Many of his poems seem to be on the periphery of those lives he had touched, his parents, his aunts, the guardians of his childhood, as though some intimacy had been denied him.

It's all in the loneliness of childhood but it stayed with him all his life. There is a craving for intimacy in his work, an extension of the childhood dream of inclusion. His poems are populated by labouring men who work by 'the sweat of their brow'; cattle drovers, train drivers, farmers who lived with the buffeting of wind, the force of rain, the nudge of animals in a field. If I were to compare him with another poet, it would be Thomas Hardy. He was an arch romantic.

However, he was far from 'dreamy' when it came to the promotion and presentation of his work. His late coming to poetry was spurred by a revulsion against the world of thrust and success, in which he had, paradoxically been so successful, both in journalism and university teaching. His early training in the offices of newspapers and news magazines gave him an efficiency in organising and circulating his work. I benefited from such professionalism. We were equally ambitious for recognition. But more than that, we were poets in a hurry, late starters excited by our early success. We were also encouraged by the marvellous reciprocity of the Irish reading public, their generosity of response to the poet, their willingness to listen and to read.

In 1998, Ted died suddenly in his sleep. We had spent ten most fruitful and fulfilling years together. They were among the sweetest of my life and, speaking for Ted, also of his. Only days before he died, he had remarked on that "very happy life" we shared. In retrospect, I think it was a deliberately affirmative comment. Sensing death, he seemed to withdraw from life, and I was angry with him for giving into what I thought was a melancholy indulgence. But now when I read his last poems, they seem full of that foreboding. They are unbearably sad: 'A Sinner Dreams of Bees'; 'The Last Suit'; 'Valhalla'. For the last four years, a group of writing colleagues have been meeting for monthly workshops in our apartment in St Stephen's Green. These meetings still take place, and Ted remains a much loved, ghostly presence.

The Last Suit

In the men's department
of Clery's, the pensioner
shy of what he's doing
asks for something dark,
then feels satin lining
around his shoulders,
and the trousers like boards
down his legs,
and he will tell
the fitter if he asks
the suit is for a christening.

Ted McNulty (*Rough Landings*, Salmon Publishing, 1992)

Sheila O'Hagan

September the fourth

At four a.m. today my lover died.
He didn't reach for me or call my name,
Dreaming he would waken by my side,
But turned his face and shuddered as some shame
Or haunting shook him and his mouth gave cry
To a portentous and unearthly pain.

Between darkness and dawn that cry of pain
And nothing warm has touched me since it died.
An ethos of cold starlight I can't name
Possessed my love while he lay by my side,
Something strange, unhuman, born of shame.
He had not said goodbye, called out or cried.

Some ghost or spirit left his mouth that cried
Out and he'd gone from me, had gone in pain
Into an alien world, yet as he died
He drew my spirit to him, gave her my name.
Something possessed him as he left my side.
His face was turned away as though in shame.

I took his absent face and murmured shame
To that which claimed him, for my love had cried
As though some shady trafficking in pain,
Some curse or Judas-kiss by which he died
Unknowingly in another's name,
Had come to term as he lay down beside

The one he loved. Perhaps lying by his side,
Fearful in sleep, I had called up that shame
And he, my love, unknowingly had cried
Out in redemption for another's pain,
As though a chosen victim. My love died
Because some curséd spirit took his name.

Sheila O'Hagan

For he was loved and honoured in his name
And I, as I lay sleeping by his side
Guarding his innocence, knew of no shame.
On the stark cusp of dark and dawn he cried
Aloud so strange my heart burned cold with pain.
Not one warm thought has touched me since he died.

Still I call his name. All hope has died.
My unspent love's my pain. I have not cried.
Such is winter's shame, all's bare outside.

Ted McNulty

Valhalla Blue

A sailing ship
paints herself on canvas
as she edges
into the grey wash
of a harbour ablink
with reds and greens
that sway along a channel
now crossed with masts
as if the brushes of those
who paint new heavens

And as she recedes
drawing herself smaller
lines the evening sky
with burning orange
as I listen to the radio
that tells of a search
along the southern rim
for rare pigments,
lost colours of legend –
the yellows of Nirvana,
the Valhalla blue

September 1998

A Sinner Dreams Of Bees

Not sackcloth for penance
but this coat of bees

Deserved, the waiting
for the first sting
when the hum in the fur
rises from a murmur
surges with purpose
then settles

Deserved, that my coat
grow heavier in each meadow
as I head north
where the coat
will fall in the cold

Now see me in my camp
circled by evergreens
and in a snow of light,
I wear the black coat
of wax, fur, wings
they left me

Something's New

Niall MacMonagle

2001 is around the corner and the Leaving Certificate examination has become our very own space odyssey. The old Leaving prescribed a standard dose of *Lear*, *Hamlet*, *Macbeth*, in various stages of bad health, mental or otherwise, and shaped the collective consciousness of sixty thousand or more students in any particular year. More so than any other country An Roinn Oideachais has been unique in shaping the hearts and minds of the young generation through its antiquated one syllabus one exam set-up. Traditionally childhood was seen as a totalitarian state whose population was not allowed decide its future; the modern student is allowed the right to choose from a wide variety of texts shortlisted by the teacher whose own input and experience will be crucial. There was a time when economic and other circumstances dictated our choice, or lack of it, but prosperity has allowed us to indulge our appetite for an endless variety of taste i.e. a cup of coffee must now be prefaced by labels like espresso, latte, cappuccino. In theory, every English class in the country will be studying its own choice of texts from titles as diverse as *Who's for Patagonia* by Bruce Chatwin, *Strictly Ballroom* by Baz Luhrmann, *Antigone* by Sophocles or John McGahern's *Amongst Women*.

The selection of texts is crucial and should in my opinion depend on whether they enrich and inspire students, crossing the threshold into adulthood, to stay with books for the rest of their lives. "If a book is well written it is worth reading" is a fine criterion to judge a book by, but for many young people choosing the right book can mean the difference between a dutiful laboured experience and an exciting, stimulating one.

While that old Leaving Certificate English course was being taught and examined, Ireland itself experienced extraordinary social, cultural, moral changes and many works written since 1970 are now options on the new course. Every play, poem, novel is a sign of its time. The young people of Ireland who welcomed in a new millennium were different in their thinking and in their outlook from the pupils who studied for exams thirty or even ten years before.

Televisual, more open, more tolerant, more streetwise, pupils now sit down before their teachers in classrooms with different agendas and different expectations and the works they are now invited to read are more varied than ever before. When Heathcliff swore he said "D---", now a prescribed poem contains the sectarian shout of "Fuck the Pope!" And if anyone is uneasy about this it is certainly not the seventeen year old.

Many of their teachers, I include myself here, were from the *Beowulf* to Beckett stable in that we graduated with a Map of English Literature in capital letters. We knew where to dig for Anglo-Saxon foundations, we had travelled to Canterbury with Chaucer's pilgrims, we knew how the Romantics had responded to the Augustans, we visited *The Waste Land* and waited for Godot. We could put the pieces together chronologically and the pieces seemed to fit.

Since then many universities have reinvented and re/deconstructed their courses. Modules on the narrative of slavery, gender and politics, critical theory created a buzz. The map was being redrawn. Flexibility became the norm. The canon was exploded. Prescription of a kind was suspect. The word 'great' was viewed with suspicion, unknown and unread works were reprinted. Political correctness triumphed and gender balance had to matter.

It is difficult if not impossible now to say that every student should read/study/know this or that text. We can all name a favourite but if I were to insist on teaching *Pride and Prejudice* or *Great Expectations,* I could do more damage than good. Roddy Doyle's favourite book is *David Copperfield* which he re-reads every five years but even Roddy Doyle might experience the familiar frustrations known to everyone when an attempt is made to convey one's enthusiasm for a nineteenth century novel or in Henry James's words a "loose, baggy monster" to a resistant, indifferent audience.

We have never been given so much choice as teachers. The texts have literary quality and one text will suit some not others; some will come to admire them as the year goes on but the emphasis, it seems to me, should be on not what is taught but on how it is taught. If a book can be looked at for what it is in itself and seen within the context of its time and of ours then the thinking which surrounds that book is open and positive and stimulating.

In school I read essays by Bacon, Hazlitt, Stevenson, Lamb, Newman. These were dropped. I regret that, but only when I think of those students blessed with a particular kind of intelligence. Perhaps another level, an advanced level beyond the Higher and Ordinary Level would allow for a more rigorous course of study for a very small number. Elitist it may be but who suffers when a minority is willing to go the extra mile. To continue the sporting metaphor – what sports enthusiast is dismayed by the high achiever?

If no list at all were made available, if young people themselves were to choose, John Grisham and Jilly Cooper might emerge as frontrunners and poetry might be dropped altogether. All pupils come to learn that there is, in Michael Longley's words, "the beauty of things difficult". Why eat fast food all your life when there are other more challenging, sophisticated but ultimately rewarding tastes?

The challenge then is to persuade them to experience texts that they might not otherwise hear about or read and to convince them that an initially difficult or strange text reveals itself and yields its riches if allowed to. The advantage with this new course is significant. Many of the authors are not only alive and well but are continuing to produce extraordinarily fine work.

It is well known that world literature has been reduced to two plots: a stranger comes to town or a person goes on a journey. This is a comforting thought when faced with the question of what story would interest a seventeen year old? And the world they know about is often so limited. Sometimes it is the strangeness and otherness of the experience that will excite and stimulate. Seamus Heaney's good advice is for teachers to "stand up for strangeness, the otherness and challenges of the stuff."

Few teenagers will know married love, what it is to poison a partner or the horror of solitary confinement and none of them will know what it was like to be a butler in a stately home in England in the 1950s but Donne's *The Anniversary*, Eugene McCabe's *Death and Nightingales*, Brian Keenan's *An Evil Cradling* and Ishiguro's *The Remains of the Day* allow us to experience vicariously these different worlds.

But what to teach? Something old or something new? The impulse is for the immediate, the contemporary. Let's read Roddy Doyle and Irving Welsh. But then we listen to this:

Niall MacMonagle

Westron wind when will thou blow
The small rain down can rain
Christ if my love were in my arms
And I in my bed again

The ache and longing in those lines are eight hundred years old and they can be felt now. Shakespeare's plays bring us back four hundred years but they really bring us to ourselves.

The thinking within the universities has filtered through. Secondary school English syllabuses in Ireland are now coloured by what has been happening at third level but also at second level in other countries. The old essay style question is no more. The compartmentalising of language into five different headings – narration, information, persuasion, argument and aesthetics – makes for clearer thinking. Reading and identifying such genres and writing in similar mode should make for a sharper, more aware school leaver.

The literature paper is also innovative. A long list is offered from which four texts are chosen. One of these must be studied in depth, the other three will be compared and the lists will be different each year. Film is also on offer but the NCCA in devising the new course missed a wonderful opportunity to give film the attention it deserves. Why not a choice incorporating a proper film studies slot?

Poetry is now studied differently. Instead of being invited to read, say, fifteen poets, the number is now limited to eight at higher level but these are represented by ten poems each. Poetry, as it is to be examined, alas, is still unsatisfactory. If I had my way I would have a wide variety of poets and poems in one anthology. Read many poems by many poets and focus too on one Irish, one English and one American poet, to be studied in depth. I would also discontinue the idea of the 'which poets will come up syndrome' that has tainted the teaching of poetry in this country for the past thirty years. Some students since 1971 have opted to study only the Anglo-Irish poets (yesterday I heard a chap in Dunnes Stores tell his fellow shelf-packer "Don't bother with anyone but the Anglo-Irish"). Next time around similar narrowing and uneasy-making thinking will happen – if it isn't the Anglo-Irish then the women poets should be a safe bet. Let the students read all the prescribed poems and then choose which poems they like best. If allowed to write on what you like best then you will produce your best writing.

Niall MacMonagle

What I see as the most valuable thing about an English literature course is both assurance and otherness. Both the familiar and the strange are encountered. And Ezra Pound's advice to teachers is vital: "you must like the young people you teach more than the subject". A passionate interest in literature is clearly essential and a belief in its power to create a special space within the reader where a thought might grow are important but remembering those young people are carrying with them their futures and ours is the most important lesson of all.

Eavan Boland was recently asked how she would teach her own poem 'The War Horse' to a class of seventeen year olds. "Begin with the horse," she said. "Don't mention the word 'poem'. Go to their own experience of horses or their lack of experience of horses. Work out from there." Now there's some good advice. Put the horse before the cart and you're on your way!

A Few Notes on Genre in Poetry

Giovanni Malito

The word 'genre', borrowed from the French, originates from the Latin 'genus' and means race, type or kind. This word, 'genre', puts me in mind of the Swedish naturalist, Carolus Linnaeus (1707-78), who is more remembered as a taxonomist. Linnaeus introduced what is known as the binomial system of nomenclature for the scientific naming of species of plants and animals. And the word 'scientific', as used here, might be replaced with the word, 'precise'.

Hence, any modern poet is biologically known as a member of *Homo sapiens*, genus and species respectively. To take such classification into the area of what the poet writes is not a simple task. Whatever boundaries exist between various sets of movements and/or historic periods in the arts is ill-defined. Classically speaking, however, the major literary genres were epic, tragedy, lyric, comedy, and satire, all of which applied directly to poetry, with the newer forms, novel, drama, and short story, being added later. Thus, we could have classifications like Epic poetry or Tragic novels. There can also be a further and quite clear distinction made between 'Genre of Poetry' and 'Genre Poetry'; and this is something that relates directly to the ongoing and forever fruitless debate concerning 'form versus content'.

The genre of a poem hinges on the form in which it is framed and/or composed. That is, its actual structure is delineated on the basis of set rules that govern things such as line count, line lengths, stanza configuration, etc. When the prescribed rules are followed then the various types of poetry produced are not easily confused. A limerick is excessively different from a terza rima. However, the Ten Commandments aside, rules are not written in stone, and nor should they be. Poetry must be an organic entity, but the arguments that follow upon any changes in the rules are sometimes nothing more than inane. For example, there is a current debate in some of the English journals as to whether or not any poem consisting of fourteen lines should be called a sonnet. Who cares?

Fortunately, in the case of genre poetry, the form does not matter. It is completely optional because what defines the genre in this case, is the content of the poem, or what the poem is about. Unfortunately, this opens up a new can of worms. For example, the subject or theme may clearly be of a spiritual nature, but it may not be

Giovanni Malito

clear whether the actual poem is a Religious poem, a Sacred poem or even a New Age poem. In some cases, one might even confuse any one of these three categories with Pagan poetry. On the other hand, some genre poetry is fairly easily identified, and one of the oldest types fitting this description is Love poetry.

Examples of Love poetry written in any of the known forms, ranging from acrostic to virelay, abound. Modern Love poetry still often appears as sonnets, but more frequently as free verse or in one of the Eastern syllabic forms (haiku, tanka, sedoka, sijo, etc.), which have been rapidly gaining popularity in the West. Still, Erotic poetry, which concentrates on sex and sexual love, is sometimes confused with Love poetry, which tends to avoid sexual details although there are exceptions. Another new genre, Gay and Lesbian poetry, usually tends toward overlap with either or both Love and Erotic poetry.

Although it is not nearly as prevalent as its prose cousin, the Horror story, Horror poetry is another readily identifiable genre. The themes are the same in either case. At the moment, Horror poetry might appear to be slightly more restricted in form than Love poetry, but this is merely due to a renaissance in Gothic and neo-Gothic writing. In fact, one could consider Gothic poetry either as a sub-genre of Horror poetry or as a separate genre altogether. Another offshoot, and an extremely popular one in the underground press, is Vampire poetry, but Horror and/or Macabre poetry, are necessarily more far-reaching, extending well into the psychological domains. Thus, Horror poetry need be neither restricted in structure nor limited to subjects like ghosts, ghouls and zombies. Not all Horror poetry being written today is doggerel, although almost all of the Cowboy poetry I have read to date definitely is.

Beat poetry, a relatively new genre, is a distinct product of the Beat movement, haphazard as it was. Beat poetry can sometimes overlap with Jazz poetry as each of these are written in contemporary idiom and are meant to be read out loud. The term 'beat' in this context has been ascribed to Jack Kerouac, and bears connotations of down-beat, off-beat, down-and-out, drop-out and beatitude. The original Beat writers of the 1950s actually went beyond idiom and developed a slang of their own. Individual poets like Kenneth Rexroth, Allen Ginsberg, Gregory Corso, Lawrence Ferlinghetti, and others, each possessed highly idiosyncratic styles, but generally, their convictions and attitudes were unconventional, provocative, anti-hierarchical and anti-middle-class. Nonetheless, neo-Beat poetry, perhaps too popular on the United States small press scene, should not be confused with the political and/or polemical Anarchist poetry for which a separate and rather large underground market also exists. Protest poetry is yet another distinct genre.

The early Beats were primarily influenced by Zen Buddhism, Amerindian and Mexican Peyote Cults, and by Jazz music. Jazz poetry, another specialist field, often occurs as biographical narratives or even elegies about famous jazzmen, and tributes to musical instruments, in which cases the poems are usually written in 'normal' free verse. But when the poems are devoted purely to sound, Jazz poems can be among the most structurally adventurous poetry written today. In fact, from the beginning, Jazz poetry was devoted to sound, and was always meant to be recited to the accompaniment of jazz music. Although this is thought to have initiated with the ballads of Vachel Lindsay (1879-1931), it was not until the late 1930s that poets like Langston Hughes and others really began to collaborate with musicians.

Some poetry works better on the stage (Performance poetry) whereas other poetry works better on the page. And then, there is poetry that can only work on the page. In this category is by far the most structurally avante garde of modern genres, Concrete poetry. The term 'concrete' as used here does not signify 'normal' accessible poetry, as according to some writers/critics who employ this word, so to avoid any potential misunderstanding, the term Concrete/Visual poetry will be used instead. Although it is tempting to say that Concrete/Visual poetry came out of movements like dada and surrealism, it actually harks back to the altar poem. The latter, also known as the 'carmen figuratum', or shaped poem, is believed to have been first written by Persian poets of the fifth century. In an altar poem the verses or stanzas are arranged such that they form a design on the page that takes the shape of the subject of the poem. A classic yet modern example would be *Vision and Prayer* by Dylan Thomas.

Concrete/Visual poetry more often than not exaggerates the shaped poem concept to such an extent that the poem is the picture produced. Perhaps there is an echo here of Marshall McLuhan's *The Medium Is the Message*? In extreme examples, pictorial typography will completely displace verse sense, syntax and grammar. Poems in this category are produced on all kinds of media, from paper to stone, and might even be completely devoid of words, composed instead of numbers or other symbols. Journals that publish Concrete/Visual poetry also tend to publish other works of so-called "experimental" poetry, ranging from found poems to intricate texts and sub-texts, serious descendents of the more classical Nonsense verse of writers such as Lewis Carroll and Edward Lear.

Finally, although it sounds a contradiction in terms, Science Fiction poetry has been steadily gaining prominence since before World War II. In 1938 Arthur C. Clarke had lamented: "Strangely enough, little progress seems to have been made in the writing of fantastic poems, in spite of the fact that verse is probably a better medium than prose for expressing the ideas of Fantasy and Science Fiction". Clarke should indeed be pleased that there are now many entire publications devoted to SF poetry, and in a large number of these there is much inevitable overlap with both Horror and Fantasy poetry. In fact, in some circles, the term, Genre poetry, immediately signifies the trio of Horror, Science Fiction and Fantasy poetry (H/SF/F). Although SF/F poetry is very difficult to define, it can be said that generally its themes are the same as those for SF/F prose which essentially break down into four categories: Hard SF which is linked to the hard, or physical, sciences; Soft SF which is linked to the so-called soft sciences, i.e., sociology, psychology, anthropology, etc.; Science Fantasy; and Fantasy.

Sometimes, what is known as Science poetry, which is among the most difficult types of poetry to market, is also included with H/SF/F poetry. I am surprised that with all the lipservice we constantly pay to modern science and technology that there is not more Science poetry being written, or published. And one need not be a scientist to write Science poetry. W.H. Auden once suggested that all poets subscribe to *Scientific American*. Section 44 of Walt Whitman's *Song of Myself* was obviously based on a voracious reading in contemporary science. Perhaps, the problem is that Science poetry tends to appeal to the intellect rather than to the emotions?

Of course there are other genres that have not been mentioned here, but the point is, one can write about whatever one wants to write about. There is a name for it somewhere, if you need that kind of security, and whether or not you want to split hairs over the precision of the name is up to you. What I know is that there will be interested readers for anything you write, provided of course it is written well. And to write well, one must read well and widely. Let the content come to you, and the form will come to the content. And, if you break up these last few sentences into phrases, put them in short stanzas, you will have an example of Didactic poetry. Interestingly, it has been argued that all poetry is, by implication, didactic. It should and does instruct, but will not necessarily delight and/or move the reader. Spontaneous manifestation of the latter is what separates penmanship from writing.

A Genre tanka Cycle
our legs
intertwined
softly rubbing
putting crickets
to shame

> I'm happy
> so shoot me and
> freeze this moment forever
> or else come back
> in about three hours

his cheeks deflate
the red leaving them
emptying his spit-valve
he closes his eyes
slowly for the Adagio

> tribal sounds
> and the boom of drums
> the young ones are out
> getting old tonight...
> I'm getting younger

and what is it
that lies beyond this joy
of your lips parting
that makes me fear
for tomorrow

> on the moon
> there is a bible
> opened to Deuteronomy
> and no wind

Big MAN Beat

Me and GOD
have got a good thing going
I call on HIM in the morning,
admire his flowers & trees
HE'S got great nature.
We hang out for a while.

Sometimes HE calls by
in the day
when I'm least expecting it,
we drink tea together;
hang out, I bring out cakes –
GOD loves my baking.

In the evening,
leaning over the garden fence
we share the sunset,
shoot the breeze.
that's when HE shows off most.
MAN, the sunsets we share.

HE has a little place right next to me,
I call round whenever I like,
HE calls his place *Elysian Fields*:
HIS bit of a joke; but better than calling it
Dunromin. And anyway, he hasn't. Me either.
We've got a good thing going –
me and GOD.

Mary Pound de Rachewiltz

Fresh and unfussed you came from Brunnenberg
in the Alps to lecture at Maynooth for the
Gerard Manley Hopkins Summer School.
Your father never owned a book of his poems
finding the metrical labours "unduly touted".
"It can't be all in one language", you quoted his dictates:
debtless to Robert Bridges but not to Hardy
who insisted on getting the subject matter first
and agreed with Maddox Ford about freshness of language
and fought Yeats for changing the natural word order.

"And for those who deform with iambics..."
the theatre seated less than fifty and afterwards
you showed your translation of the *Cantos*
into Italian plus Canzoni, you smiled
and tucked up your head proudly
"And do they cohere?"

What about his years of incarceration? Ezra was
a bad boy and had to pay his debt to society.
But, the head shifted and the jaw turned on line
with your shoulder, he speaks to us from the
silence of the final fragments. I can still hear
his diatribes on money, banking and interest
rates; "and to know interest from usura" your converse
peppered with his poetry as you signed the bulky tome
that is his epic of some length, below your name adding
daughter – translator. Then a lecturer, Irishly said
"there was only one Ezra Pound" to which
the vice-president of the college smirked
"one was enough."

Kevin Kiely

Ted & Sylvia
from *Plainchant for a Sundering*

Drove West that year in the beat up Uno
a tick compared to our manic high. O'C's Superstore for
supplies, the pub two Guinness, a rock band cranking
out Rory Gallagher's *Morning Sun, Walk on Hot Coals.*

The double cottage chill owned by well-off friends, the
attic where we sank hot whiskeys and offered our
bodies at the Feast of Lupercal, tantric gods peeped
through loosening roof-boards.
Dawnlight a small bird flown down the wide chimney
and perched on the hand-rail
the kitchen Aga choked in ash, smoke and bad moods
hills ridged with trees, one ridge higher, bound
in by smooth peaks – a kind of Irish Colorado.
The stove in the backroom studio used turf, so too
the open hearth beside which Taizy began a
self-portrait after Raphael, one eye centred staring.
On solitary short strolls, my sight through the window
of her image peering back.

For days cocooned
in the twinned house a passageway and dividing doors
my pecking at a keyboard and she called wanting
to release her innards, the indecision, the impossibility
of capturing what is or might be out there, or was
it some interior no-self that mocked her in the mirror
outstared her from the canvas spinning into dizziness?
We struggled – it must have looked as if we were
trying to stab each other until
a tinny rattle and the pallet knife hit the stone
floor. Why not get at the dark stuff in her wrists
she'd longed to open paint in veinfuls? Our faces

white in the mirror with bits of hills and foliage
and the sky outside where we went gaping in the
moments when talk is useless.

Our walk came upon a
trapped ram, horn-hooked to a willow, four legged
creature suspended by crown stamping in his muddy
ground. We released him into the rain, blown back
as if sweetly when he revelled in new found freedom.

Day floated on day, we tried Mount Aigle holy
mountain of the Druids and fell back tired, hungry
damp and cold for the comfort of the car, a far
off thumbnail of blue below us at one point. Then
the radio announced Ted's death and the *Times*
next day quoted how at their first meeting Sylvia bit him.
The imagery of her as frightened fox cub, the
children, his infidelity that sliced the marriage.

Kevin Kiely

Passenger
from *Plainchant for a Sundering*

Late train. Empty carriage in pre-sunset effulgence
My face reflects indecision as images of the children
haunt my boarding at Coolmine. The train gathers speed
and shakes the gut with fear. What is a breakdown
but a bridge to something once it's not an exit from life.
Nettles, blooming valerian, fences of wild parsley
fly past the windows. A shower hoses the glory of
flowering weeds, clumps of buttercups with yellow teeth
child's teeth after eating candy. Dog daisies whiskering
from an overarching bridge, the train slows down
beside clusters of damp tissue paper
poppies yellow and red.

These are a sleeping pill but train travel can activate
sharp bends on the mind, strange areas of the head
The children are almost visible down a long tunnel
beyond bats and murky light and voices, rustling whins
and raked pebbles, water hits the eaves of the carriage.
The train's metal seems to groan under bathfuls
of rain flung from above. Fear death or try to.

Connolly Station and the girdered undulating roof leaks
flooding the platforms. The view of the unroofed world
beyond is silt silvered, when did our marriage first
spring a leak? Clouds and early May heat the air.
The train sleeks in marked BRAY and unfolds in green
to let out and in late night commuters. Some converse
engaging each other like a good novel, others nod
and listen. Nothing could be more real, alive and
Repetitious as this journey. At Blackrock the sea sucks
beyond the station wall. The train goes on, coaches of hope
and aspiration into the dark trailing two red lights.
The little children shift restlessly half-deserted
The mind's furniture is thrown around.

Touch – A Soul Unto the Poet

This grasp of you
touches me, feeling in
places previously unknown.

First, my right hand to yours
then left, of centre
you balance me.

Lifting my heavy beams
that shouldered despair
in a *real-friend* less life.

What we forge
amid pain, delight (among other emotions)
are links going on in trust
for what each does.
Choices
led by a heart-sun.

Now, to your instillment
I can lead my dream
To a new Literature

Noel King

The Poet's Gift

Anticipating another poem of yours
I put myself in quiet,
sip tea and smoke,
feel each syllable,
the fit of each line,
dig deeper meanings,
your life.

Here is my home
solace, through your eyes piercing mine
from the sleeve of your one volume.

In years to come:

I will walk beaches with you,
but so few times
each exchange will imprint itself.

I will deliver a paper on your work
but how to vocalise your depth,
that each day shows anew,
your ever growing love core?

I will be forced to sell your
hand written works from my box
that your awkward, arthritic fingers
crafted in delicate scratches.

I will still pound across lined pages
with weak hands,
rejected

I will model your style
and live content
passing on
your gift in life.

Seán Ó Faoláin: A Man before His Time

Maurice Harmon

When Seán Ó Faoláin published his autobiography *Vive Moi!* in 1964 many people were surprised to discover that he came from a poor background. Ó Faoláin portrays the penury and restriction of home, the anxiety about respectability, the extreme piety and the loving blackmail that drove the three sons to work hard at school so that they could rise in the world. What surprised those who read of his origins was how much he had changed. By the sixties he was a sophisticated cosmopolitan who went abroad three or four times a year, wrote travel articles on Italy and America for the prestigious *Holiday Magazine*, and went on lecture tours to American universities where he was occasionally a writer in residence. To meet him in those years was to encounter a man of the world who was attractively courteous, interested in current affairs, and informed about contemporary literature.

As a young man he had been deeply affected by idealistic nationalism. When he was a university student he joined the revolutionary movement and has left a vivid description of how it felt:

> Never will I forget the first day I stood in a field, in a deep glen, somewhere to the southwest of the city, with a score of raw recruits, being given my first drill by some older students, while along the two hills overlooking the glen other Volunteers stood on the lookout for police and military... It was an autumn day of sun and shower, and just as he began to speak to us a faint, gentle sprinkling rain began to fall on us, and then the sun floated out again and sparkled on every leaf and blade of grass as if some invisible presence had passed over us with a lighted taper, binding us together not only in loyalty and friendship but in something dearer still that I am not ashamed to call love. In that moment life became one with the emotion of Ireland. (*Vive Moi!* 135)

We may feel sceptical about those blessings from nature but his commitment to nationalism was whole-hearted. Later he tried to understand that emotional attraction. His first collection of stories, *Midsummer Night Madness* (1932), relives his participation in the Anglo-Irish War and the Civil War. It moves from the delicate romanticism of 'Fugue' which evokes the traditional figure of the Irish rebel on the run, to unflattering portrayals of rebels in violent, unscrupulous action.

His first novel, *A Nest of Simple Folk* (1934), sees the Easter Rising as an explosive event that disrupted normal life. Its final section recreates Ó Faoláin's early years – the policeman father, days at school, the importance of religion, the tyranny of respectability – all of which are blown apart when young Dennis Hussey decides to join the rebels. Why does he do it? What is it that causes him to reject what he has known, to rebel against his father, to leave home and religion, to upset his mother? Throughout the novel revolution is a throbbing presence, a heritage that passes from generation to generation. While most people devote themselves to making a living and rearing families, the rebellious few are drawn to violence. Dennis Hussey feels the call and rushes off to join the rebel cause. When he examined the issues again in a biography of Countess Markiewicz he came to the conclusion that all those who had joined in the fight were driven by emotion, not reason. Apart from James Connolly none of the rebels seemed to have given serious thought to the kind of society they wished to create.

The Civil War and the reality of independence brought them down to earth. "They lived their most vital years", Ó Faoláin wrote later, "at the peak of the excitement and they fell after that into the pit of disillusion" ('Emancipation of Irish Writers', *Yale Review*, 1936). It was that sense of cataclysmic shock that drove Ó Faoláin into ever-widening and ever-deepening assessments of Irish life and history. In article after article he tried to make sense of political and social life. Even in the mid-twenties he had begun to see that the revolution was more than a political affair. It was also social. A new society was born. A new Ireland emerged from the mists of idealism – a middle-class, predominantly Catholic society with the pragmatic, non-idealistic values of the middle-class. A generation that had fought, now wanted peace in which to enjoy the benefits of revolution. As far as Ó Faoláin could see there was little attempt to formulate a desirable vision of life, some goal, some vision of the future. If the country had fallen into apathy and if it lacked direction, it needed an inspiring leader. That was the cry at the end of the opening story of his second collection of stories, *A Purse of Coppers* (1937), called significantly, 'A Broken World' in which the narrator has been moved by a priest's vision of a whole society. The story concludes on a wave of longing:

Maurice Harmon

What image, I wondered, as I passed through them, could warm them as the Wicklow priest had warmed us for a few minutes in that carriage chugging around the edge of the city to the sea? What image of life that would fire and fuse us all, what music bursting like the spring?

What had happened to Irish society? How could it be lifted out of apathy? The stories in *A Purse of Coppers* are about failure, about failed revolution, about the absence of vision. A character in one of the most delicate stories, called 'Admiring the Scenery', declares, "Every man lives out his own imagination of himself. And every imagination must have its background". Man has a right to fulfilment, to opportunity, to a context of living in which he can fulfil his potential. In *Bird Alone* (1936), Ó Faoláin used the disappointments of the post-Parnellite period to mirror his sense of failure and indirection after the Civil War.

Since contemporary Irish society did not provide a vision of a desirable life, Ó Faoláin turned to the past. He examined the life and times of previous leaders, of Daniel O'Connell and Hugh O'Neill in particular, men who had also lived at a time of social breakdown, when one society had collapsed and a new society had to be imagined, defined and brought about. Such men had creative imaginations. They had intelligence. They were open to ideas from abroad. They saw what had happened or was happening and had the energy, determination and knowledge to do something about it. Daniel O'Connell became a hero for Ó Faoláin. "In body and soul, origin and life," Ó Faoláin wrote in *King of the Beggars* (1938), "in his ways and his work he was the epitome of all their pride, passion, surge, and hope – their very essence." He was above all, he claimed, "the greatest of all Irish realists, who knew that if he could but once define, he could thereby create...He imagined a future and the road appeared." This is exuberant rhetoric, but within the mystique lies Ó Faoláin's basic belief: the true leader must use his brain, must see clearly before he can create something new and different.

Ó Faoláin uses historical biography to create model portraits. In O'Connell, as later in *The Great O'Neill* (1942), he is identifying values and qualities, ways of behaving, kinds of leaders that he feels are lacking in his own time. He admired O'Connell's inclusive, non-sectarian outlook and his definition of the relationship that ought to exist between Church and State. Since post-revolutionary Ireland had become narrow and sectarian, Ó Faoláin held up O'Connell as a model, and feeling that the

Catholic Church had too much influence, he pointed to O'Connell's liberal view that Church and State should be kept apart. Although he had, he said, once revered Eamon De Valera "this side idolatry", he grew impatient with his vision of a Catholic Gaelic state that left out "everything that was magnificent and proud and luxurious and lovely."

The historical biographies show an Ó Faoláin deeply engaged with Irish life. His work as editor of *The Bell* magazine from 1940 to 1945 is another aspect of that involvement. When he started *The Bell* he wanted to provide an outlet for the voices and interests of the new Ireland. Contributors he insisted, should write about what they knew, what they had experienced, what they had seen.One of the things least remembered about *The Bell* is the variety of its articles on such subjects as orphans, slums, prisons, country theatre, women in public life,censorship and the law, the life of a country doctor, nursing, and so on. Men and women who knew what they were talking about wrote the articles. Although he wanted to avoid politics, in the end he could not avoid them and it was his sustained, personal engagement with contemporary issues that many people valued and with which his name is often associated. Month after month in the final years he criticised the middle class, the Church, the Gaelic League, the GAA ban on foreign games, puritanism, Jansenism, bad taste, censorship. He introduced new ideas and promoted them by frequent repetition. He explained present developments in the light of history.

At the heart of his approach was the contrast he saw between Ireland before the revolution and Ireland in the 40s. He deplored the country's inward looking, defensive posture, the uncritical acceptance of all things Irish. He admired O'Connell and O'Neill because they were outward looking, because they sought to bring in new ideas from the continent. By contrast the leaders in his own time, he thought, were conservative and narrow. They feared change.

In his last attack (June 1945), on the Ireland that had emerged under De Valera, his idealism, passion, social conscience and indignation find eloquent expression. It is an apologia – for himself, for writers, for the Irish people:

> The truth is that the people have fallen into the hands of flatterers and cunning men who trifle with their intelligence and would chloroform their old dreams and hopes, so that it is only the writers and artists of

Ireland who can now hope to call them back to the days when these
dreams blazed into a searing honesty – as when Connolly told the
wrecked workers of this city that he found them with no other weapons
but those of the lickspittle and toady and that his job and theirs was to
make men of themselves. Surely these are honourable steps to follow? It
is the nature of writers to have a passionate love of life and a profound
desire that it should be lived in the greatest possible fullness and richness
by all men: and when we see here such a wonderful raw material, a
nature so naturally warm and generous as the Irish nature, so
adventurous, so eager, so gay, being chilled and frustrated by constant
appeals to peasant fears, to peasant pietism, to the peasant sense of self-
preservation, and all ending in a half-baked sort of civilisation which,
taken all over, is of a tawdriness a hundred miles away from our days of
vision – when we see all that we have no option but to take all these
things in one angry armful and fling them at the one man who must
accept them as his creation, his reflex, his responsibility. In a nutshell,
we say that this is surely not the Ireland that Wolfe Tone would have
liked to live in, or Dan O'Connell, for all his peasant coarseness and
cunning, or the aristocratic Parnell, or any man like that old eagle John
O'Leary, or the warm-hearted James Connolly, or any man who really
loved men and life, and we accuse it.

Once when I told Ó Faoláin I admired the amount of work he had accomplished in
that period he disagreed. As far as he was concerned the best years came after he had
left *The Bell*.

He relished the later years when he travelled frequently to London, France, Italy,
America, when his short stories appeared in leading American periodicals, when he
was admired by writers, academics and editors. He thought of living abroad but his
instinct was to return to what he knew. He could not jump off his own shadow.If
the stories in *A Purse of Coppers* focus on frustrated lives, those in the succeeding
collections are progressively more relaxed, more indulgent of human foibles,
endlessly delighted by the complexities and contradictions of human nature. 'The
Man Who Invented Sin' recreates the simple pleasures of young people learning
Irish in the Gaeltacht, whose Edenic happiness is spoiled by a suspicious priest who
sees occasions of sin in their pleasures. 'The Silence of the Valley' evokes the

wonder of Gougane Barra and with it the vitality of the old storyteller whose death signals the disruption of the links he had provided between old and new Ireland. 'Lovers of the Lake' uses the Lough Derg pilgrimage to explore how two adulterous lovers respond to its moral imperatives. The stories become more reflective, more delicate and compassionate in their revelation of humanity and some become allegorical. 'A Touch of Autumn in the Air' has a magical, lyrical quality. 'Love's Young Dream' is a poignant recreation of adolescent uncertainties and intuitions. 'An Inside Outside Complex' about the theme of never-ending, never-satisfied idealistic pursuit perfectly reflects Ó Faoláin's mature personality. He pursued ideals and loved life. In what he wanted for Ireland – a liberal, tolerant, non-sectarian republic in the French tradition, a country that did not fear influences from abroad, a people who would take their place with confidence amid the nations of the earth – he was before his time. Ironically, much of what he wanted has now come about.

Table Talk
(for René Agostini)

We did the paper work
then settled in
to coffee, croissants, talk of poetry.

Then he was off. To his bay tree,
bird table, a light that turned
his mind about itself.

Hearing night hawks,
finches at dawn, old reliables –
love, heartache. Ces plénitudes.

Maurice Harmon

Golden God Golden Woman

You come upon them near the Temple
standing close to the caldron's fumes,
fanning incense over head and hair,
palming it into faces, chests, arms.

One woman with an insistent air
clutches the vapour in both hands
trains it over her small breasts,
thrusting it into her bones.

When she discovers the golden man
she comes alive, caressing
head, face, chest, belly, thighs,
so intimate he seems to glow.

Will this god respond to love
so unashamed and personal,
this need, this passion,
or will he turn to stone?

Colm Toibín's Irishness

William Wall

The recent Ó Faoláin weekend at UCC was interesting for a number of reasons, not least because it was the occasion of a rare visit to her father's native city by the novelist Julia Ó Faoláin, of whose work I am an unqualified admirer. Colm Toibín also spoke, and made what was, for my money, one of the most trivial contributions of the weekend. I'm not referring to his paper, which was surely a good one but which I missed because I went home for my lunch, but to a reply he made to an enquiry from the floor about Ó Faoláin's book, *The Irish* and modern notions of Irishness.

Mr Toibín declared his wish that "all Irishness should disappear, vanish", and he accompanied the statement with a brushing gesture made with both hands and even puffed up his cheeks and made a small plosive sound indicative of a bubble bursting. The declaration fell on a completely unresponsive audience, but was later taken in low dudgeon by Dan Mulhall who advanced the images of Irish music and All Ireland Final as samples of indomitable Irishness. Toibín countered with MTV. A small outbreak of verbal fencing followed but petered out for lack of any clear definition of the issues involved. The academics, as academics do, sat on the fringes mentally registering the occasional palpable hit and managing to look indifferent.

I suspect that the question arose out of a remark of Ó Faoláin's, which we had all just heard but which was made originally in a television interview of the 1960s. He was asked if he saw himself as an Irish writer. Ó Faoláin's reply was the logical one and provided the answer to Colm Toibín's fashionable dismissal. It was that nationality is a kind of dye in which we are all immersed.

Mr Toibín *is* an Irish writer. Those young people (and indeed people of Mr Toibín's vintage) who watch MTV are also Irish. It is nonsense to suggest that a fifteen year old from Baltimore (Cork) and a coeval from Baltimore (Maryland) are watching the same MTV or hearing the same music. The world is fashioned by our experience, and while we may choose what to experience we cannot, in any more than a marginal way, affect the way we experience it. Environment and history, nature and nurture, have shoulders to the door of perception and their combined weight is substantial.

William Wall

Mr Toibín's rejection of whatever definition of Irishness he wishes to revile is so typically Irish as to be boring. For years the All Ireland Finallers have been characterising it as West-Brit, Mid-Atlantic, Returned Yank, etc. We in the authentic districts (Rebel Cork, The Kingdom and certain islands) have seen it as typical of the Dublin Jackeen. It is cater-cousin to Shoneenism and sworn enemy of the gombeen. And if all this sounds a bit stage-Irish that's because it is. Handy Andy would feel at home with it, as would Hardress Cregan, Captain Boyle and Bónapart Ó Cúnasa.

Other nations have the same problems. Two French talking heads are just as likely to be disagreeing about encroaching Americanisation. The Germans, from time to time, get completely twisted about the German national character. Americans have expended quite a lot of energy in establishing what is un-American. Perhaps one of the defining features of some national characters is an obsession with the difficulties of defining national character.

At any rate I return to Seán Ó Faoláin's admirably simple statement of the reality. We are all washed in the dye of Irishness. Factional selections of elements of that dye have, to mix metaphors, added vitriol to Irish politics for generations. David Trimble's choice is to call his kind of Irishness *British*. Charley Haughey felt himself so quintessentially Irish that he bought an island as far away as possible and put his money in an even more remote place. Kevin Myers takes the view that Irishness involves a willingness to lay down your life for your near neighbour, and so on. There is, at the very least, standing room for all-comers.

I'm not sure, because the acoustics were poor, how Colm Toibín looks at it. He can hardly see himself as American on the sole ground that he watches MTV. Perhaps he sees himself as international: he certainly travels a lot. However, killing off his origins is going to involve a great deal more than sniping at the All Ireland Finallers on their way up for the match. Besides, these same gentlemen (and, typically, they are mostly men) have shown themselves quite capable of shooting back.

In the meantime it must be said that the whole debate provoked yawns from the people at the Ó Faoláin weekend, whose attention was drawn to the more arcane issues such as whether John A. Murphy really said that UCC was right not to appoint Ó Faoláin to the chair of English. I suspect people were a little embarrassed. One lady from the audience summed it up on our behalf. "We didn't respond," she said, "because we didn't think he was serious."

A Plain Country: Ireland in the 1950s

Eugene O'Connell

The 1950s is one of those unique decades that belong somehow to an older Ireland; Anthony Cronin called it like the last decade of Medieval Ireland, and yet it spawned modern masters like Samuel Beckett, Seamus Heaney, John McGahern, and Brian Friel, who still return to it – some at a gap of fifty years – for inspiration.

The decade kicked off predictably enough by naming 1950 'Anno Santo' (The Holy Year) and the weather forecast was as ever predictable: fresh south to south west winds with cloudy occasional rain at first, but fair periods, and scattered showers likely to extend eastwards later in the day, becoming colder. The papers were full of the communist take over of China and the churches added the souls of that vast nation to its prayers for the conversion of Africa. The country was saturated with 'Black Baby' boxes where the head of a child sat on top and thrust itself forward and then back obligingly when you put in your penny. Edna O'Brien pictured this motion as analogous to a throbbing penis in her novel *The Country Girls* and was castigated from the altar and of course duly shunned in her native Clare.

Heinrich Boll, the German novelist who visited Ireland in the mid-fifties, noted the multitudes who visited the cinemas that seemed to spring up even in the middle of bogs in Kerry and Mayo with windows daubed in green paint, he also remarked on the heavy rain in Limerick. The 'Situations Vacant' columns of the paper were short and rather quaint – one spinning company looked for "Girl Twisters and Reelers" – and factories in England wanted Irish female operatives.

Ingrid Bergman was suing for divorce in California and there was talk of abortion in the Continent, but the news that eggs had dropped from 5/6d to 3/6d a dozen must have troubled the rural housewife who saw her pin-money dwindle. More ominously the finance companies, then unregulated, advertised "Cash Advances from £5–£100, with or without security and cash in the Strictest Privacy". There are no bank advertisements, though historians now tell us their coffers were full of savings.

When Dorothy Lange, the American photographer, arrived in Ireland in 1954 to photograph the country for *Life Magazine*, it rained for fourteen weeks of her stay;

Eugene O'Connell

though she was cheered by the Irish temperament. She snapped a 'travelling man' one day near Cratloe and noted that photo to be the truest representation of Ireland of all the 2,400 photographs she took. Heinrich Boll noted in his *Irish Journal* that the roads were full of donkeys, children, and these "travelling men". These vagrants slept in hay barns and in the lofts of the odd house where they brought news of other townlands at a time when travel was limited and people rarely moved beyond their parish.

1954 was the 'Marian Year' when grottos, modelled on the original at Lourdes, sprung up everywhere and *The Song of Bernadette* became the favoured drama of the strolling players who put up a tent or fit-up in the village green and doubled up in various parts to entertain the locals in the manner of a bad *Bull Island*.

In a letter to America at the time Nora Keneally described Ireland as "a plain country but still quite happy" though there seemed to be a curious embargo on fun. Frank O'Connor accused the Irish police of shadowing courting couples in *Holiday*, an American tourist magazine, and a priest in Kerry parked his car on a timber ramp that had been set up at a crossroads dance in a desperate attempt to counter the dreaded habit of company-keeping. The pubs closed at ten though there was an incredible rule that if you lived more than three miles from a pub you were classified as a visitor and allowed to drink to any hour, one can only imagine the desperate journeys that were to be embarked on as closing time loomed. The national radio station which did not start until half past five in the evening was called *Athlone*, after an obscure Midland town that no one ever visited and it broadcast a staple diet of news, Irish language, opera and the occasional song for hospital patients. It closed down at eleven – though it was switched off an hour before that when the country knelt down for the rosary on a concrete floor that was sloped to drain excess water so that the population stood at an obtuse angle and slightly off-kilter to the world.

The age of fourteen was one of those emblematic or rite of passage years that signalled the end of youth and the beginning of work except for the privileged few who went on to study for the professions. They would service the farms, sleep in the loft and work for their food and twenty pounds a year if they had hired themselves out to a good farmer. Dorothy Lange, who had witnessed the extinction of the Californian dirt farmer during the 30s saw a strong parallel with the fragile

Irish subsistence economy. She feared for the future of the Irish tradition of kinship with family and land epitomised in the tradition of Cohering where the 'boy' was lent at harvest time to help the neighbour. Heinrich Boll had already noted the crowded farms and wondered at the ability of the country's narrow industrial base to absorb the surplus. Local historians have noted that this feverish activity was a last gesture of defiance at a state that would allow fifty thousand of its number to emigrate every year.

And yet the 'Up Dev' sign in Clamper, (near my own home in North Cork) had only to be touched up every four years and did for every election; though one local headmaster in Glash School posted a map of the London underground in his classroom in open defiance of the local inspector to guide the 'Big Boys' who would be leaving. The abandoned villages he saw in the west of Ireland, and the curious silence at his inquiry as if the story of these departures had somehow been deliberately lost, fascinated Heinrich Boll.

Anthony Cronin wrote in his editorials in *The Bell* at the time, of a collective death wish that seemed to hang over the Irish nation. Samuel Beckett was probably nearer the mark when he wrote in *Murphy*, the first novel of Irish emigration, that the Irish had no interest in history or tradition and would destroy their own heritage as if they were a homeless or exiled people in their own country. I remember wondering as a child at the returned emigrants in blue serge suits with a carefully cultivated wallet in the back pocket and at why they walked past the ball alley into the pub and drove to tourist places like Torc in Killarney, as if they had become foreigners in their own country.

The word 'delicate' had a curious resonance in the 50s and denoted a sickly or consumptive person or somebody with a 'want'. These people were an embarrassment to the ideals of the Saorstat and were despatched to various institutions like the 'Mad House' on the Lee Road. This was the largest building in Europe and was full to the brim, though some of these people were kept at home to service the needs of the household and rarely wandered beyond the kitchen door. It was perhaps ironic that these 'ainniseoirí' or forgotten people were the first to be given a voice by Samuel Beckett, one of the modern masters, in *All That Fall* and *Waiting for Godot*, where the tramps are mirror images of the vagrant or travelling men that Beckett saw as the true inheritors of the Spailpín or poetic tradition who were ousted from their lands in the eighteenth century and condemned to a life on the road. The early novels of Beckett were banned and a radio broadcast was suppressed in the mid-50s after which he retorted that "Ireland doesn't give a fart through it's corduroys for art".

The summer of 1959 was one that felt it didn't belong to the fifties at all; it was long and hot and the mood was upbeat. The 'poetry wars' had abated in Dublin and even Anthony Cronin was optimistic at the news that a new press (Dolmen) was publishing genuine Irish voices. The first tractors had arrived on the farms, television was opening a window to the world, and the new aeroplanes had shortened the Atlantic route to three hours. They drove Dev out to the park and a new and bullish breed that included Lemass, Kinsella, McGahern and Heaney, got down to work to invent their version of an Ireland that would bring us into the twentieth century.

The Glass Purty
(for Bernard O'Donoghue)

Say it was Lisleehane in the Glass Purty
When you shook it and not Lourdes,
With the snow pouring on its dreaming spires,
And you raced over fields for the cows
Instead of through an Alpine village,
Stopping for breath in the sharp air
To bathe your feet in the warm dung,
And Mary Anne was the only vision
To greet you on the journey home,
A shawled Mannequin with a basket
On her way to the Egg Man with her hoard.

Eugene O'Connell

In Jones' Wood
(I.M.D.J.C.)

What does it mean
To hear that Cuckoo again;
More than the realisation
That shook you into recall,
Of how some ancestor of his
Must have boomed his note
Out of that same wood
And stopped your labour that day,
So that you rose with the company
To ease the ache in your back,
And trace between smokes the history
Of the Jones' in these parts,
Before you bent again to hear the Slean
Slicing through the bog and never thought,
That next time your visitor would sing
Out of these woods to you alone.

Dancing at the Digital Crossroads

Donal Horgan

Crossroads, a term loaded with De Valerian overtones, may not readily come to mind when considering the digital revolution. Perhaps some Euro-Fund metaphor like roundabout or overpass, while not exactly appropriate to the needs of the Irish dancer, might seem like a more apt term given the pace and extent of that same digital revolution.

It may be a cliché but nevertheless it's true: technology has transformed the way we live. Everything from making a phone call to making a bank transaction hinges on the technological revolution of the last twenty years. For some, technology has become the religion of our age. As in all religions, there are the out-and-out fanatics who are convinced of the ability of technology alone to solve most human problems.

Looking at one group of technically literate (but socially illiterate?) end-users, namely compulsive mobile phone users, it does not always seem as if technology is there to serve us. Fashion statements aside, it often seems as if it is the people who are there to serve technology and sheer gadgetry. As Umberto Eco famously put it: "It is the person with power who does not have to answer the phone." One can only conclude that there are a lot of powerless people in today's world.

Technology may be neutral but the culture associated with it certainly is not. This is especially so in Ireland. Advertisements for computers (even those by Irish companies) invariably come with American accents. It may seem like a small point but nevertheless, it carries with it the subtle implication that all things Irish are inferior to a largely American-orientated techno culture.

This view is essentially a technological view of technology. It locks in on a particular mechanistic view of the world, one normally associated with America. It fails to recognise just how central creativity and the human imagination have been to the digital revolution itself. As it has developed in sophistication, this same revolution has come to rely more and more on a world of symbols and icons. The curious thing is that nowadays when people express a difficulty with new technology, chances are the difficulty is in operating in a world of symbols and icons as opposed to 'button-pressing'.

The connections between an 'old' Ireland and the new silicone glens straddling the M50 may not be apparent at first. In an Irish context, the word 'imagination' is something of a loaded term, more usually seen as the domain of the true artist dutifully starving in some garret while waiting for artistic inspiration. While we are all aware of the role of the imagination in a literary and artistic sense, we often neglect the real connections between creativity and technology, especially its role in problem solving and technological development. The human imagination lies at the heart of the digital revolution. If Ireland is a hub of the digital age then it may have as much to do with people's ability to operate in this new world of symbols as any narrow 'technical' skills.

The human imagination provides a key insight into something that is inseparable from new technology – human behaviour. While technology strides ahead, very often it is the human application of these technologies that is as important as the technologies themselves. The human application of new technologies may be quite different from those suggested by the technologies themselves. Knowing and appreciating this is not just some fascinating piece of trivia – it can be the difference between success and failure in any undertaking.

In this context, the impact of technology on big business looks certain to change the way we shop. This is evident already with banks planning to move many of their operations away from the High Street to online services. This has resulted in the peculiar phenomenon of banks with expanding fields of operations and profits planning to close anything up to half of their branches. Such a scenario would have been unthinkable as recently as five years ago!

An area greatly neglected in all of this is the impact of the digital revolution on the state. The Nation State, that entity from the nineteenth century over which two world wars and countless other wars were fought, may well be unrecognisable within twenty years. Change has already come in the form of de-centralisation, with whole sections of the Civil Service being shipped box by box from Dublin. The next wave of change is imminent with a question mark being placed over a whole layer of government and officialdom – that of the information forwarder and bureaucrat. Given that more of our legislation is coming directly from Europe, the days of the pen-pushing civil servant may well be numbered.

Donal Horgan

In an age of commercial globalisation, the notion of the global village may seem somewhat redundant. Ironically, it is technology and especially the Internet that have made the local more important. By overcoming the problem of physical distance, it has de-emphasised existing national infrastructures in favour of worldwide local connections. The geography of the future may well be built as much around URL addresses as the place names of old with all their associations of history and literature. It may yet herald the re-invention of the local world.

Human beings for all their high-tech gadgetry remain much the same as they've ever been. They tend to be creatures of habit and routine more inclined to the known than some mythical cyberspace fast-track. Technology alone will never solve problems but combined with the power of the human imagination, it can go some of the way towards it.

Standing at the digital crossroads, the imperative now is to put the human imagination centre stage. This may not always be in the best interests of big business and especially the IT business. However, it is most certainly in the best interests of people. In time, this may turn out to be the difference between dancing and dancing to the tune.

Cracks

Maybe our romance was smouldering
Anyway when we moved in.
But soon, jagged cracks broke through
Our bedroom wall's fresh green.

We argued. Repainted the wall.
In vain: the cracks grew wider, deeper.
So we sealed and plastered them,
Covering up with paper.

Which seemed to work. Until that last,
Clouded summer when through the wall
Dark stains spread where the cracks had been,
Exuding a musty smell...

And what good is it now to know
It was all just heat-rifts & soot
Seeping from an old chimney breast
After the fires died out?

Padraig Moran

The Dark Road

Work-bound now, I no longer bide
The town's snail-like traffic jams,
The stasis at the right of way;
Where a huge "Finches" soft drinks ad,
Showing an empty cage, proclaims
Go on. Set your spirits free!

Instead, I go by the short cut
Popularly called The Dark Road,
Which I knew in my dancing prime
As a secluded courting spot:
Cars nosing in, gravid with dream,
To seek the dark at Knox's wood...

Now, mile by mile, through bumps and muck;
Past hard-hat men felling the trees,
I drive, more tense as school looms near:
Another day of trying keys
To Wordsworth, Yeats, Dickens, Shakespeare;
Of urging, *Take up your pen and walk.*

Another day of scribbled notes;
Of raw voices; red biro ticks;
Of minds sunk in apathy.
Unbridgeable gaps. Culture shocks...
Again, I face the graffiti
Makers, the stragglers through the gates.

Fool of the Family: A Look at *A Life of J.M. Synge*

Carl O'Brien

In 1907, Irish society was scandalised by the mention of a female undergarment in a new Irish play. *The Playboy of the Western World* was the play in question and its author was John Millington Synge. In this biography of Synge's life, W.J. McCormack traces his career from "Parisian scribbler into a world famous dramatist".

J.M. Synge is not an easy subject for biography. Much of his life remains shrouded in an obscurity that reflects his elusive character. Synge enjoyed the company of many associates but had few intimate friends. He had a passionate interest in Ireland but remained largely non-political. He was at ease in peasant society while remaining a distinct outsider. He is remembered as a dramatist but his early loves were linguistics and classical music. His visits to Aran, beginning in 1898, were later viewed as pivotal to the cultural revivalist movement. In reality, Synge was probably just as much influenced by his walking tours of Wicklow as his rather short Aran excursions.

John Millington Synge was born into a middle class, Church of Ireland family in 1871. At the time of his birth, the family resided in Rathfarnham and later moved to Orwell Park in Rathgar. The Synge family had a long tradition of service to the church and a senior branch of the family retained a family estate at Glanmore, County Wicklow. However, by the time of J.M. Synge's birth the family were no longer prosperous. Synge's widowed mother was largely dependent on the rentals from poor Galway holdings.

The early life of the playwright and his unremarkable studies at Trinity College, Dublin provide little by way of anecdote for the reader. McCormack compensates for this lack of personal detail by providing the reader with an in-depth study of the Anglo-Irish society in which Synge played little more than a nominal role.

His leanings towards agnosticism and his disinterest in conventional careers marked out the young Synge from his immediate family and their society. In 1893 he travelled to Germany to indulge his love of languages and classical music. These cultural holidays along with wintering in Paris and walking tours of Wicklow, established a pattern of lifestyle which Synge chose for most of his adult life. A rejected proposal of marriage to Cherie Matheson, a young woman of strict evangelical upbringing, further distanced Synge from the narrow social milieu of his upbringing. Nevertheless, he maintained a close bond of affection and loyalty for his family and particularly his mother.

Synge was viewed by his family as a disappointment. His seemingly unfocused lifestyle contrasted sharply with that of his brothers: one a medical missionary in China and the other an engineer in Argentina. It is little wonder that conventional society viewed him as the "fool of the family".

Synge's first visit to Aran in 1898 was later celebrated as a great cultural event in the Irish literary calendar. However, the timing of the visit may be of greater significance than the place itself. Synge was still in despair following his rejected marriage proposal and the Hodgkin's disease, which would kill him, may have already been diagnosed. Synge went to Aran to learn Gaelic and was referred to as 'duine uasal' by the islanders. He visited each year from 1898-1902 for a period of four to six weeks on each occasion. His first visit provided inspiration for *Shadow of the Glen* (1903) and *Riders to the Sea* (1904) as well as a book on the islands.

Synge enjoyed the company of the islanders but he had no desire to mythologise them. His notes testify to his intelligent insight into island life, which he understood to be capable of both great kindness and great cruelty. This theme would work its way into his drama and is perhaps personified in the relationship between Pegeen Mike and Christy Mahon. Synge's contact with peasant life also gave him occasion to meet young women in a setting less formal than the drawing rooms of South County Dublin. Sexual need and desire is another great theme in his work. His notebooks testify to his appreciation of the sexual candour of his island guide and the beauty of the island girls. However, his rather obsessive love affair with the actress Molly Allgood influenced his female roles in *The Playboy of the Western World* (1907) and *Deirdre of the Sorrows* (1910) more than any island beauty.

Synge's mature work coincides with the period immediately after his last Aran visit and continues until his final illness in 1909. However, it should be viewed as the culmination of a lifetime's experience rather than exclusively inspired by his island excursions. His linguistic interests and his readings of Ibsen's peasant dialogues should not be underestimated in their influence on his work either.

J.M. Synge's body of work provides a deep and rich insight into the Irish psyche. Many of his themes still have a resonance for Irish society today. *Riders to the Sea* developed images of loss and hardship. *The Shadow of the Glen* provides a radical view of emigration, madness and illicit sex. *The Playboy of the Western World* questioned family values and moral truths. *Deirdre of the Sorrows* seems to echo the long troubles in Ulster.

W.J. McCormack's excellent biography allows the reader to assess Synge's important contribution to Irish drama and his unsentimental portrayal of Irish identity. Nevertheless, despite McCormack's efforts Synge remains something of an enigma, which is perhaps fitting for a man who moved quietly through many different worlds.

A Night of Light

Alice Taylor

The trees in the wood above the village were slowly gathering their dusky coats around them. Along the street the shadows were drifting into doorways from which people emerged all heading in the one direction. The celebration of the 'Last Light' ceremony was about to be held in the Church of Ireland church at the western end of the village. On the way into the church people took time to sign the *Millennium Book*: a specially bound leather book embossed with gold lettering, 'Innishannon Millennium Celebration, 31st December 1999 – 1st January 2000'. The book was to be a record of all those present in Innishannon on this historic night.

Inside in the church people gathered in the dying light. Christ Church, built in 1856 is the seat of Church of Ireland worship but tonight the congregation of St Mary's Church joined them in strength. People continued to pour in until every pew was overflowing. The churchwarden Joy Scanlon succeeded in procuring seats where none seemed available and all were made to feel welcome. When the incoming tide turned to a trickle it was decided that the ceremony should begin.

A delighted Canon Burrows welcomed all, expressing his appreciation of the large numbers. He rose to the occasion with a meaningful ceremony befitting a special time. His theme was that 'God's time is now'. Some lights had been left on to guide people to their seats but now these were turned off. The church was in darkness. Slowly three people: Gabriel Murphy, Mary Nolan O'Brien, and Maria Callnan, emerged from the back porch and walked up the aisle bearing a large candle. They were members of St Mary's congregation bringing the gift of a tall Jubilee candle. They placed the candle on a centre table where Canon Burrows lit it with solemnity. The light was carried to the candles in the windows and then it slowly spread along the pews as all the little Millennium candles fused into light. The church was a glow of yellow candlelight and voices were raised in songs of praise as we all sang from the same hymn sheets.

Afterwards people drifted very slowly from the church as if reluctant to leave this communal pool of peace. They bore their small Millennium candles homeward. Some waited to sign the *Millennium Book*, which had not been possible on their way in. As they queued they chatted quietly. The Jubilee candle was left lighting in the centre of the church where it seeped soft light up into the arching rafters. On the Gothic windowsills candlelit floral arrangements pooled light along the now emptypews. As we walked down the sloping path from the church the flickering candles danced shadows through the stained glass windows.

Later that night the still lighting Jubilee candle was brought by three members of Christ Church up to St Mary's church on the hill. They carried it along the street passing their old family homes: Elizabeth Hawkins O'Sullivan, May Beasley Giles, and Joy Buttimer Scanlon. At St Mary's, Fr O'Donovan PP and Fr Hughes CC who led them in procession to the altar welcomed them. Twenty-four people each followed the candle bearers, carrying an emblem of a parish organisation that they represented. On the steps of the altar were six people ranging in age from the oldest man in the parish at ninety-four, to one of the youngest at four months. The light was passed down through the ages and then down along the church. The small Millennium candles glowed for the second time that night and the dark church was turned into a sea of wavering candlelight. Members of both churches did the readings and voices were raised in songs of united praise.

Afterwards the lit Jubilee Candle, carried by members of both communities led a candlelight procession down the high hill into the village and along the street to the parish hall. Our local guard Donal McCarthy went ahead to slow the traffic. It was a night for our village to move at its own pace. The parish hall was transformed into a wonderland. Lighted candelabras graced tables of food and flowers. A giant Jubilee candle in a sea of Bogdale dominated the centre of the hall. Bogdale alone could equal the millennium in antiquity. A brilliant creation in blue and silver, the millennium colours graced one corner of the hall and in front of the stage in pride of place stood a tall elegant grandfather clock. Tables laden with soft drinks, wines and eats occupied one side of the hall. Children helped themselves to party food. All the goodies were made and sponsored by locals.

As the hour of midnight approached all gathered around the clock. The countdown led by Paudie Palmer began. It was a heart gripping moment! Suddenly the time was upon us and it was almost too momentous to absorb. The doors of the hall were thrown open to hear both church bells ring. The soft background music in the hall changed to mellow dance music and people decided that it was dancing time. And so the hours were danced away and photographs were taken. It was a night to be held in cameo. Our final ceremony was a simple sharing of unleavened bread and wine with the Jewish member of our community. As we left our parish hall we wished that we could hold the day and 'Night of Light' forever in our minds.

Introduction to the winners of our Short Story Competition
David Marcus

One factor that distinguished this year's competition from those of earlier years was that, despite the accustomed intriguing variety of themes and styles, in the end only a relatively small group of stories displayed the virtues that made them realistic contenders for the three awards, and in that group just three stories stood out ahead of their rivals. Very likely the slightly smaller number of entries than usual brought this situation about, but I wouldn't, at this stage, consider the reduction a worrying development. I believe that other short story competitions have also suffered a drop in entries this year.

The number of entrants with definite writing talent was noticeably greater than those whose stories made the final list, and so it may be useful to suggest, briefly, factors which inexperienced writers should keep in mind when writing a short story. First and foremost, remember that it's a short story, so compression is vital. There's no room for over-detailed scene setting or character descriptions. It's the story itself that counts, so its core element should be implied or made clear very early and unfolded from then. Secondly, don't have too many characters. Two or three main ones is an ideal number: any more raises technical difficulties that require a well-developed, experienced technique or a much longer story than is advisable or normally allowed in competition. Finally, don't be complicated and don't write melodramatic, purple prose passages. Remember that in a short story what is left out is often more powerful than what is put in, that is don't over-explain. Something that the reader can imagine for himself needs only to be suggested, not meticulously described. Point the way, but let the reader supply his own detail.

As to the three stories that came out on top this year, they were, in the order in which I first read them: *A Compact Disc*, *Gas Man*, and *Swans and Spanish Trawlers*.

A Compact Disc: An unusual story by an obviously practised writer. A man and woman who have known each other since childhood are lunching at a restaurant. He has just been ditched after a five-year gay relationship with her brother (who was kept by him, but who has now got an excellent post in an orchestra and has taken up with one of its players). The man is a lawyer; the woman, highly educated, has studied a number of courses, including one on relationships. She believes he was exploited by her brother and needs help, needs to understand that his easy and calm acceptance of the break-up is misconceived.

The story is not really about the break-up but is a portrait of a very loquacious, dogmatic, arrogant, even obnoxious woman who is annoyed that the man will not accept that her brother exploited him. It is a well-crafted story, but a jarring incident with a waitress seems to have been inserted as a plant for a not really successful ending, and a reference to Bach's *Goldberg Variations* suggests it is an orchestral work when in fact it is a work for keyboard. These objections apart, the story displays real originality, sharp characterisation and excellent dialogue.

Gas Man: A delightful, intimately told and expressed story, about Fineen and Anne-Marie's fourteen-year marriage relationship. Ostensibly a huge dead and rotting whale that has floated into a cove near the fishing village where Anne-Marie bustles about the B&B she runs, propels the story. Fineen rows out to the cove and ties up the whale, deciding that if he can cut it up and save its ribs, he could make a week's wage in a day. The difficulty involved and the fact that the imprisoned whale's stench is causing objections in the village, force him to forget his plan and float the fish out to sea. But the story's insidious counter-theme is the sexual relationship between Fineen and Anne-Marie. She, being a confirmed believer in God's and the church's laws, allows Fineen his conjugal rights only when she's in a woman's way. Fineen is thoroughly frustrated and rails against God, his *gas man.*

Sea and sex, a formidable combination, provide the not always smooth rhythms of Fineen's life, and his difficulty in striking a consistently

David Marcus

sustainable tune out of them, makes a story that in its irresistible writing
and treatment never strikes a wrong note.

Swans and Spanish Trawlers: Dano has lived in the small fishing village
all his life, fishing from his trawler, but now that he's over sixty, he
knows he has only a few years work left. After that he has little to face.
Fishing and the sea have been his world. Excellently built atmosphere,
setting and pace, mirror Dano's semi-philosophical temperament, and
the wonderfully effective writing matches his sleep and dreams with the
rhythm and movements of the waves as he trawls for prawns.

In his catch he finds a massive crayfish, his favourite fish, and his
motivation for returning it to the sea is very affecting. But the ending,
his suicide, is in my opinion a mistake. We know, as mentioned above,
that he has little to look forward to. A suicide ending leaves nothing to
the reader's imagination, but in this particular short story I felt that a
more reflective ending would have provided a very satisfying added
resonance.

After a number of re-reads and much cogitation, the placing I finally
decided on is as follows:

First:	*Gas Man*	**Chuck Kruger**
Second:	*Swans and Spanish Trawlers*	**Amanda Norton**
Third:	*A Compact Disc*	**Paul Brownsey**

Gas Man

Chuck Kruger 1st

From the kitchen garden Fineen spied it, a short solitary stretch of thick tannish-white foam heaving with barely discernible swells at the mouth of the inner harbour. He rubbed his eyes, looked again: no, no foam line, no apparition.

"Stop," he muttered. Last night'd been what Ciarán, his Boston-based big brother, had learned him to call a 'wing doozy'. Anne-Marie, no, she weren't speakin' to him. He'd heard nothing but battened-down silence in the steamy kitchen. He'd raised his knife and fork upright, his freckled fists either side of the place, but she'd taken his gesture literally, had bustled about brusquely, as if to say she was after fitting his breakfast in 'mongst her main chores – caring for three B&Bers in the dining room and preparing martyr-like the mixture of Sow Breeder and table scraps for the saddlebacks – and here it was going on eleven, Jesus, Mary and Joseph.

When she'd turned on the Pat Kenny show, he knew she'd roll away from him that night too. Ships passing. Hoot hoot. Long Fastnet foghorn hoots. Yeah, eerie, relationships. Tangled fishlines. Longlines at that. Sometimes you just have to cut bait. But they don't teach you that in school, not here, not then. Just inform ya like the church, don't, don't, don't. How to untangle, you God, you goddamn God you.

He could suddenly not remember what her inner thigh looked like, felt like, once white as pollack flesh, smooth as a slippery buoy. Fourteen years married. Sure he might as well, tonight, go out. Bloody hell but a chat in the pub's people, a night at home's TV. But not for more than the count of eight; ten and you're out, my good lad, and out's out and ye be one scrapper of a boyo.

Fineen came fully awake, found himself alone on his lookout point, the alien foam breathing there before him. He walked back, as if a young man in his determined and rapid head-down stride, fetched the battered binocs from above the dresser, returned to his favoured spot above the sea, and trained them on the patch. Its middle rose and fell oddly, languidly, twelve to fifteen inches above the gently breathing sea. He imagined a curtain of tide bearing him a gift.

He decided to give Anne-Marie's garden weeds another afternoon of reckless freedom – the kind in which he stoutly believed – and sallied forth to investigate, grabbing a pair of oars and spurs from the shed.

Five minutes later he leaned over a bollard, around the base of which lay his chain, padlocked. The swollen top of the bollard prevented his loop from being lifted off by the idle curious. The chain stretched ten feet out over the harbour, there attached to his stern line, the new blue rope not yet stained by algae. Too much taut tension from the boat and bow anchor for any eejit to pull the chain in, undo the knot, help themselves to my punt, thank you very much. He saw a contradiction, remembered the swish of a certain soutane, growled, "Some people don't know no *don't*, others don't know nothing but."

He fitted the key, ready for the increase in tension, and, with the released mooring line, pulled in his red-gunwaled punt, leapt aboard, fitted the spurs, began bailing. The bilge water smelled of mackerel.

He cast off. Back into the oars, back into the harness. He felt good rowing, valued it, as if it were a friend: you know right where you are with it, no mystery; you can count on it to do exactly what you want it to do. No moodiness in an oar, by God. I could've been born with an oar in me hand. Better than a silver spoon in the mouth. An oar for a sceptre. If kings had calluses wouldn't the world be steered!

He feathered the oars even though there wasn't a puff of breeze, establishing rhythm, and it wasn't but ten strokes before he felt he'd always been rowing. He loved losing himself in a sense of rhythm, yes, but damn Anne-Marie's rhythm, each stroke, or lack of stroke, a nail driven home. Coffin. Fetters and freedom. The point, not just to finish, to lay ahem the slates, to have the roof watertight, to conceive boom diddle-oh, but to climb back inside each whack of the hammer, to listen to the sound as it goes up the scale, the nail first long and deep, short and shrill, in and home, next please. Oh for a family of fifteen, not this modern conservative everything-in-its-right-place bit, damn the rhythm method, but sprawling, neat when necessary, say on Sunday, but unkempt and spontaneous too, just to live now and then in an all-of-a-sudden way, like now, like off again God knows where, the devil. And give the old boy his due. Under the oxters too.

He twisted to check his progress. A hundred yards to go. One end of the patch looked considerably narrower than the other, the whole thirty-two, thirty-four feet long. Maybe, the little boy in the middle-aged man whispered, I'm approaching some treasure, some mystery floating in on the tide. Thought don't have to have boundaries, like relationships, like farms, this mine, that yours, you may go no further, halt. Danger: Bull.

A putrid smell reached him well before he reached the carcass. Whale or basking shark he couldn't determine, so rotted was the almost amorphous mass. He could tell which the head, which the tail, little else. The flesh, pitted, had a hard rubbery texture, some twisted white strips dangling down like kelp. He rowed around and around it, occasionally poking the mass with an oar blade. He laughed, said aloud, "If that porridge don't put hairs on your chest, it'll take it off. Fit for a fucking king. Fit for someone what says *don't*."

He discerned a two-foot-long fin at the base of the head, noted that the tail spread evenly apart, some five feet, that the dorsal fin had all but disappeared, that a small eye, like a pig's, looked mournfully blank.

Then the thought struck him, making him grin: if he could secure the putrid, decomposing hulk in a little cove, he could cut him up, salvage the bones. Wouldn't they, weather-blanched on the garden wall, attract the B&B crowd? Maybe sister Moira could even sell some in her craft shop, "Whale ribs: Special once-off offer: £19.95". How many ribs in a whale? And was the female made from one too? Yes, maybe them bones would rise again, pay for a kicker for the boat, fifteen hundred quid worth. Like the weeds in the garden, he saw his fanciful thoughts spread out and run riot. He knew it, could hear, as if on the muted sound system in the Skibbereen funeral parlour where he'd been for Aunt Mary's memorial service, his father's quiet refrain, "Take no notice".

He returned to the pier, to the bollard, to home, sat on his lookout point beside the garden, pondered.

Anne-Marie brought him a plate of sandwiches, a mug of coffee, said awkwardly, "I hope you're not planning on any more mackerel, Fineen. The freezer's over-full."

"No girl, no, not today girl." He looked into the middle distance.

She hesitated, finally couldn't ask him again about the garden, her garden, with his help, for she'd no back, not since Roisín, their second daughter. He in one of his mulling moods, she knew better than to provoke. "Marriage is better than no marriage," her mother had counselled her, but hadn't mentioned what Anne-Marie had come to call "them dead-end days". What, after all, did he give her? Hangovers?

He seemed, she thought, looking back, part animal. He can sit there for hours, alert as a feral cat in first light in a field and he all alert for a mouse or a vole. He did nothin' and then everything. Work, or drink, or figure out. She returned to the laundry. Or me.

He didn't turn but could see her walk off, the way her head bent slightly to the left, the way her right foot turned in the last six inches of each of its thrusts forward. But he noticed that he could not see what he wanted to see.

He trained what he called his crow's eye – his left eye had a clarity his right lacked, at least at distances – on the leviathan's tidal movements; *his* leviathan's movements.

The next day he watched a lobster fisherman who berthed beside the pier in the other island harbour motor in to the corpse, for it still lolled about in roughly the same area, just a bit nearer the far foreshore. But the man Pádraig, soon moseyed off about his business, certainly not about his father's, thought Fineen, who remembered a story of how Pádraig had used a Leader grant to buy his boat for the sake of "educational tourism". The only thing he'd ever educated was a conger eel when he broke its back for having stolen into one of his pots.

Biding his time, Fineen waited until Pádraig clambered up onto the pier to collect his second string of twenty-five pots. He asked the usual, until finally, with all the inconsequentiality he could muster, he wondered if Pádraig might give him a hand towing 'the visitor' – Fineen pointed – to a nearby secluded beach where they could cut him up, mince meat. His neighbour looked strangely at him, then grinned, suggested he hop in. Fineen told him his ideas. Pádraig looked him over again, carefully said not a word.

Once thick in the stench, Pádraig made it clear he'd help tow the whale – for whale he was sure it was, "too big to be one of them bovine basking sharks, and bony besides, and the skin not sandpaper" – but wanted "nothing else whatsoever full-stop to do with the glop". They tied a weight to a piece of rope, tossed it over the tail, fished it out on the other side, made a loop, pulled it tight around the base of the tail. Then they started towing the beast, the engine working hard, exhaust fumes engulfing the men, the massive long-dead weight behind dragging what Fineen called its nonexistent heels. Gas man.

He pointed to a sandy cove and they pulled the wreck in as far as they could, nudged it further into the shallows with the bow. Fineen hopped out, secured the rope to a boulder. If the rope held, the beast would stay put at low tide, he reckoned, at his leisure, he could cut off the flesh, separate the bones. Sell 'em, make a week's wage for a day's work.

The next morning, while putting two pounds of petrol in his car – more would bring the level up to a tiny hole in the tank that leaked going up and down the steep hills – Fineen chatted with old Johnny, cap down over forehead, who recalled that some eighteen years back, when a whale washed in, several uncles and he had cut up the tons of flesh with bread knives and collected vertebrae, still relics about the island, some bones still west of the Bird Obs, others beside the Master's gate.

Half an hour later Fineen set forth, armed with Anne-Marie's bread knife. Waist deep in stained water, he began making incisions. After three hour's surgery about the head, and succeeding in nothing except covering himself in viscid noisome grease, he had to call it a day, the tide now in. But I'll show the bugger who's who. The winter waves'll do my work for me.

He returned home, dripping, sauntered with a touch of hangdog excitement into the kitchen to have his tea and tell Anne-Marie what he was about. She sniffed him before she saw him, ordered him out out out, not in her kitchen, how could he, honestly, after all, in God's name, holy sufferin' Jesus.

"No buts," she said. "None. The health inspector'd close us down. Like that." She snapped her fingers. "The immersion's on all morning. Don't touch nothin' except the inside of the tub. And throw your clothes out the window. Jesus, Mary and Joseph, Fineen, you're nothing but a child, a little spoilt child."

"Sometimes I wish I was. I'd get more attention at night."

"You get all the attention you deserve so."

"You and your priest."

"You're not to come between me and our God."

"Why not? He's come between you and me. And he's not 'our' God. He's yours. And you can have 'im, lock, stock, and barrel."

"We've been through this, Fineen. Be a man, not an animal."

"Get off your pedestal."

"If I'm on one, you put me there."

"I've put you nowhere, Anne-Marie. It's you've put me somewhere, in a freaking limbo."

"We have sex when it's safe, and that's when I'm in a woman's way, and that's that. Period."

"And when is that period, tell me, wife."

"When the good Lord sees fit, not before. Please Fineen," tears catching light, "I won't be sinning just to make you feel good for a few bloody seconds."

"I won't be sinning just to make *you* feel good," he repeated in a snarl as he stalked off. He left the kitchen door, normally closed because of the B&B guests, open. Anne-Marie, weeping, slammed it, then stood in the centre of the kitchen, hands flat on the table, and stared at the oven door.

Two nights later, by chance, he met the temporary island nurse in the pub and they fell to talking, number six. He learned he'd run serious risk. "Had you had an open cut on you," she said sternly, "you might have contracted septicaemia. You never know what infections live in long-dead fish, Fineen. Some treasure that would have been, eh?"

And then, number seven, he heard from another fisherman neighbour that the dead whale had been on the shipping news two weeks ago, an object thirty metres long floating about the Fastnet and to be avoided. It posed a serious risk to local fishing boats.

His friend-in-arms, he knew. The bouquet was right. Number eight. Maybe if Anne-Marie wore such perfume, he joked with himself, I'd have no difficulty. That'd teach me better than any parish priest. Island man. Gas man.

The next night, no sooner had he ordered number two, than the manager of the campsite discreetly informed him, in the corner by the stairs, that that whale high and dry in the cuas was beginning to reek so badly that his campers three hundred yards downwind were complaining.

"You put him there, you move him, Fineen."

"I'm after waiting for him to rot so I'll have his bones."

"And when'll that be?"

"A month, two."

"I won't have a campsite by then but a cemetery. And no one there save the spirit of your brilliant find."

"The wind'll change."

"And it'll change again. But the stink won't change. You know, Fineen, it'd be a shame to have to take legal action. But if my campers start leaving because" – and here he poked Fineen in the chest with his stubby forefinger – "of your fucking whale, I'm going to court, hell or high water. That's the cut of my tide, my friend."

Fineen investigated at midnight, number eight or no number eight. The manager, blast his knobbly balls, he was bleeding right. Not only did a stench fill the air, but, in the light of his torch, a gauzy grey petroleum slick covered as much of the inner harbour as his light could reach. Blubber? Oil? He wondered. He'd heard stories of how his ancestors on Cape used to burn basking shark oil in their lamps. Aunt Marie, she'd sworn by it, said electricity, when it arrived in '72, weren't nothin' but the work of the devil, the same devil that had blown off her roof when lightning struck in '57. Now wouldn't that have been some sight. How she'd trembled, flesh on a stick, whenever she heard thunder thereafter, poor thing. What a bang that must've been. God's crack. Craic. Gas man. God's a gas man.

The next morning, high tide, he rowed over to the cuas, unloosed the rope, bits of flesh hanging from it. After a half hour of putting his back into it, he'd no sense of any rhythm, no Anne-Marie rhythm, no rowing rhythm, no anything rhythm, for fuck's sake. He could feel back and shoulder muscles knotting either side of his neck. Like pulling a locomotive with your bare hands, and off the track, and through the ditches.

Three hundred yards gained, sweat pouring down him, making his thwart slippery, but now back to the mouth of the inner harbour where he'd first spotted him. There he let him go, the tide having started to ebb.

Goodbye law-suit, so long treasure; 'tis an ill whale that brings no man any good.

For the next two weeks he watched his creature. It had floated calmly back into the harbour the next day, had gotten stuck inside a far cave. Let the manager do something about that, let him sue God for all he's worth. Should he stay there, he'll rot and then I'll claim the sunken bones, fish 'em up with me grappling iron. And should he was out on the tide, and the change of wind, so be it. I'll take no notice.

That thought, he tackled the garden. In one day had it weeded. On the next he started breaking ground for the new shed he'd promised Anne-Marie. He'd have the slates on before gale season started, he would, of that she could be sure.

And sure but I'll give her a bottle of stinky perfume for Christmas – just to remind me of certain god-forsaken boundaries. And don't try to sneak off, thigh. Be part of my treasure. Beach me, Anne-Marie, number one. I'm your whale, ye of the thigh bone mine. Number two. Gas Man? Me? Now who, dear brother, ain't?

Swans and Spanish Trawlers

Amanda Norton 2nd

The dinosaurs were in that night. Huge, wallowing, creaking dinosaurs. Engines spewing clouds of blackened Stone Age breath into the hastening darkness; steel straining against steel, calling in deep resonant tones to each other.

The quay was empty except around the newly arrived trawlers. There, the buzz of activity was all encompassing; frantic forklifts swirling around, carrying this and that, here and there; mammoth arctics waiting to take the catch away, back to Spain.

The man had stood watching for several minutes, seemingly unnoticed by the foreigners busy at work. He chewed on the stub end of his cigarette and in one smooth motion pursed his lips and spat into a nearby fish box. He cleared his throat and spat again. Someone looked up and noticing him raised a hand, not so much in recognition of the man, but of his breed. He was a fisherman and like knows like. His mother had named him Daniel and his father had given him his name, O'Sullivan. The rest of the town called him Dano. Dano had lived here all his life, more than sixty years. He knew everybody and he knew their business. Dano, without knowing it, was a philosopher and a storyteller, a man with very little book learning but a lifetime of education. He was a fisherman, a good one and was looking forward to the morning when the wind would drop and he could steam out past the heads, out into the open sea and fish. It brought him a strange sense of belonging, a feeling he got nowhere else. He was a true fisherman, it was his life. He was born, he went to school, had gone to sea, fished and eventually he would die.

Dano walked slowly to the edge of the pier and looked down onto the deck of his small trawler. He would sleep on her tonight and be ready for an early start in the morning. The ladder down was icy cold and covered in grease mixed with seawater. Dano didn't notice, this was normality.

As he undid the padlock and opened the wheelhouse door he felt that familiar sense of contentment and safety. Letting himself in he got out another cigarette and lit up, filling the small cabin with smoke. Later, snug in his sleeping bag in the small bunk below, Dano got to thinking about tomorrow's trawling. His mind wandered along corridors of tide, wind, sea temperature, swell and wave height, lee positions and where the other boats are likely to be. His half century of knowledge and understanding moves around like a well oiled gearbox until, when everything comes right together, he knows it'll be good. As he drifts softly into sleep, his thoughts tumble about, gently flowing around and around until finally the deep relaxing slumber overtakes him and his dreams turn to fantasies unremembered in the morning.

*

He could still see the coast in the distance, obscured now and then by the Atlantic swell and the rolling of the boat. The wind was blowing enough to make the steel rigging sing a little and more than enough for Dano to have the flaps on his hat tied tightly under his chin. He was humming as he worked, checking the warps straining away into the heaving sea in between sorting the wriggling, seething mass of sea creatures spilled out over the deck.

Dano was after prawns today and was doing well. They were coming up big and plenty of them, together with the prime flat fish struggling to avoid the thousands of claws, they would fetch a good few dollars at the co-op. He was happy. He had bacon for a feast, a carton of Carroll's and he was fishing. When he had time to allow his mind to stray from his task he thought mostly of how much he enjoyed being here; he spent time watching the little black and white birds following him, diving right under the boat and coming up the other side and he spent time just sitting and remembering way back.

After sorting the last of the prawns, Dano smoked a cigarette and drank some tea, tea almost the colour of the rusty winch, in a mug whose insides were the same shade. Starting the winches up Dano looked down into the deep water, it was about sixty fathoms here and it took a while to haul the long multicoloured net back in. It was heavier this time and full, Dano could tell by the cables that led down into the water, they closed in as the net filled up.

The little boat heaved as the big swell did its own share of bullying and pushing around. At least the net being down gave him some added stability, and it was good craic being out here when most of the smaller trawlers were still in the harbour; these young ones didn't know what real fishing was about and Dano's friends knew well enough that Dano knew what he was about.

When the haul in was finished, Dano heaved and cursed and cursed some more. He'd never seen such a catch in this net and he wasn't sure if there was enough room to empty it all onto the deck space. Finally he undid the bottom of the net and the slimy, pinching mess poured out into a huge heap.

Amanda Norton

He was still staring at the catch, drawing deeply on the twentieth or thirtieth Carroll of the day when something caught his eye. Dano was partial to a bit of crayfish for lunch and he thought he could see a glimpse of that familiar colour. He grabbed the shovel and slowly, (hanging on to the rigging), pushed the prawns around until he could grab at the crayfish.

"Jesus Christ and Mary, Mother of God" (he said it out loud – talking to himself and the air around him was quite normal), the crayfish was massive. Its tail, the bit Dano liked to eat, was at least two feet long and the rest of it even bigger. Its feelers were like two huge SSB antennae and Dano's mind began to calculate its worth. About two hundred pounds, maybe more he thought, he could buy a lot of the black stuff with that.

Gingerly, so as it couldn't grab him, Dano used the big ice shovel to lift the crayfish over into a sectioned deck space and went to brew himself some more tea. He needed to rest, the surprise of the crayfish had taken his breath away and he wasn't getting any younger. He knew he was getting weaker and slower and although still very strong in most people's terms, he could no longer work his boat the way he used to.

He carried his mug onto the deck and took out a cigarette. He'd got to thinking a lot lately about not being able to fish; he felt he was getting too old. He'd probably got three or four more years and then nothing. T.V., eating and a few friends round for the craic once or twice a week, and nothing. The thought was beginning to obsess him.

The crayfish cracked at him, waving its long antennae around in anger. Dano cursed and threw it a couple of the biggest prawns and a nice little lemon sole. He had respect for his prey and spent long hours watching them, wondering what they did down there, away from the pressures and stresses of the wonderful Celtic Tiger, away from the neighbours who talked behind your back. Dano didn't much like humanity, they'd never shown him much to be very impressed with, and they didn't have any of the natural beauty of the creature before him. He sat looking at the crayfish. It was almost as though their minds were exchanging thoughts. He knew its contentment, the calm serenity of its home and the ease with which it could feed itself. It was a very wise crayfish, it was a very old crayfish.

For the first time in his life Dano knew what it was to feel envy. He looked around him at the distant mountains, the cold undulating ocean and the clutter left behind from weeks of snacking and hundreds of mugs of stewed tea. This was his world and he loved it, but he also lived in the small town and harbour, he also needed the bank and the fisherman's co-op. He also had to listen to the constant complaining of the other fishermen, never satisfied, never contented.

He took out his packet of Carroll's and lit up, drawing deeply. The crayfish stared at him, its eyes deep with understanding. Taking the ice shovel Dano lifted the crayfish gently and lowered it into the water. As it began to sink it turned and looked back at him with knowing. It knew. Dano sat on the side of his trawler, his feet just reaching the water. He looked around behind him and felt nothing. He slid off and into the enveloping seas, following the crayfish down and into contentment. His mind knew peace. His body knew freedom.

*

The dinosaurs were in that night, racked up alongside each other at least six or seven deep. It was late and the activity of unloading long over, the crews were passing the time gossiping on deck and drinking heavy Spanish wine. One or two fed the family of swans with continental bread and cornflakes, others watched. A small local trawler was tied up at the end of the pier, strung amongst the 'for sales' and decommissioned relics. It wasn't for sale, and it wasn't fishing anymore. No body had ever been found and probate was confusing. The locals were already weaving wondrous tales of Dano's exploits and finally his end. The back stabbers stabbed and the women in the supermarket had known it would happen. There were those who blamed Dano and there were those who blamed the black stuff. Not one of the stories was as beautiful or as peaceful as Dano's dreams and a few stood near the small trawler and wondered and almost knew.

A Compact Disc

Paul Brownsey 3rd

"The main thing is," Stephen said, carefully removing an olive from his pizza and placing it on the side of the plate, "that we shall remain friends."

Deliberately, Brenda's heavy face suffused with genuine concern. How controlled he was, how emotionless, (only on the surface, of course): he might have been explaining a will to a client. She said warningly, "Stephen, you've got to acknowledge your feelings of hurt and anger."

Brenda Stanton had taken many courses, at one time or another, and had always made it clear to the lecturers – and not only the male ones either – that she was no nineteen year old, naive and insecure, but that her experience (of life, of people, of relationships) made her particularly well equipped to understand what Marx or Darwin or Plato or Jung were on about; though they did tend to intellectualise.

Stephen, she conceded, did not intellectualise now. He just looked politely puzzled, his face, at thirty-four, still incredibly boyish, full-cheeked beneath short neat blond hair. He laid down knife and fork across his plate, ends on, and interlaced his fingers above it, elbows resting on either side. She detected a flicker of hesitation before he said placidly, "Relationships do end."

She shook her head, firmly but also so as to disclose disappointment in him. "Stephen, look at your *body-language*. Knife, fork, arms, all in straight lines across your chest. You're *guarding* yourself. Because you *know* I've touched something you want to keep at a distance." She nodded to confirm it, and the way his eyes did not quite meet hers was a second confirmation.

"Anger," she said coaxingly, "is a perfectly *natural* reaction to the way he treated you. Even though he is my brother."

Joel, talking excitedly about an engagement to substitute for a sick viola player in a BBC broadcast of the Brahms' Op. 91 songs, had said, "By the way, Stephen and I are finished." His eyes shone: he always made announcements, of whatever kind, as if he expected them to delight the auditor. He added, "Do you want to come to the recording?"

"But that's *awful*! For Stephen, I mean." Nothing was awful to Joel. Indignantly Brenda realised how little she had been allowed to know, to *really* know, the quiet, invariably composed lawyer whose face could nevertheless be imagined turning sulky, though she had never seen it so. (Could it be imagined turning passionate?) That choirboy face was given to pathos by the immaculate white shirts and dark suits his profession obliged him to wear: how meticulous he could be about tidiness, cleanliness.

Joel said, "Oh, he agrees it's for the best. Will two tickets do?"

"He *agrees*..." She shook her head tolerantly at Joel. Her brother trusted people to agree with him as a puppy guilelessly expects to be found delightful. Stephen had loved Joel – yes, the word "love" was perfectly appropriate to such a relationship – with a sort of quiet absorbed intensity: obviously he would need help to get through this shipwreck. She telephoned him to suggest they meet for a meal. "I mean, I don't want you to feel that because you and Joel have parted, that you and I have to, you know, not be friends."

"I'm sure Joel wouldn't expect that."

She had hardly touched her own pizza. She continued, "Look, have you heard of Alan Rosenberg? In his book he says that in bereavement – and that's what you've suffered – literally a bereavement – there are four stages of the grieving process. First, guilt, because you think it's your fault the person has died, left you, and I'm sure it's not, I know my brother. Second, anger at what took the person away from you; you know, his new relationship, the new person he's involved with. Third, anger at the person, the dead person, for leaving you, that's the most difficult stage to handle, most people back off from it. And then there's, ah, oh yes, acceptance; you know, you can let go and get on with your life. And the grieving process has got to go through these four stages, else you can't deal with your loss, you'll be crippled. Emotionally. You've got to get in touch with your anger."

He considered this like someone who had heard of anger as he might have heard of some archaic offence still on the statute-book but never actually encountered in his professional experience, say, cow-killing by witchcraft. "Is it possible I might have gone directly to the fourth stage you mentioned?" he said, but though he attempted a smile she was not taken in by it: his eyes were anxious, telling her she was close to the place where cauterisation must be applied.

"Stephen, face it, you were taken for a ride. Exploited. Just look at the pattern. When you meet Joel he's broke, living hand-to-mouth, bits of teaching, substituting, odd weeks in the pit for amateur musicals. You give him a home – your *lovely* flat – you *keep* him, really. Then after five years he makes it, place in the Philharmonic: permanent, salary, pension, security. And what does he do? Goes off with this oboe player," – a ridiculous and degrading instrument, said her tone – "Callum, who never says a word. Well, I suppose he talks to Joel sometimes. Can't you *see*, Stephen? You were *used*. By my own brother. It really makes me choke, what he did to you."

She added, "I mean, it was your first involvement, wasn't it? Your first gay relationship. Did you have a girlfriend before?"

At an early age Joel had confided his homosexuality to her as though he had sought out and acquired the gift that must please her most. In their teens they had picked over the same youths, giggling together in a manner that had puzzled their parents and given grounds for more giggling. "Mark Ritchie has lovely warm dark eyes," she might say, and he'd say "Yes, but red hair is a turn-off," and she'd say "His lips are too thin and hard-looking, just edges to his mouth, really – you can't imagine him kissing you passionately," and he might say "Nice bum, though," and she wouldn't quite like that, even though she agreed, and so would laugh out loud.

Stephen replied in the balancing voice, which you could imagine giving a dispassionate appraisal of the strengths and weaknesses of a client's case, "Things could have been difficult once Joel got into the Philharmonic. They do tour a lot. Callum is probably much better for him. He knows the stresses and strains of a musician's life as I couldn't. Possibly I wasn't sufficiently sensitive to his problems." His slight formal smile was compromised by a string of mozzarella between lips and plate that he seemed at a loss to deal with: oh, it was unfair that there was nothing she could do to help.

"Low self esteem," she sighed. She twirled the windmill shafts that were a feature of the 'Pizza-Best!' pepper mill. "It's what destroys so many relationships. You can't feel your anger because you feel you didn't deserve Joel's, well, love in the first place and it's just *natural* for you to be dumped. Stephen, you've got to believe that you *are* what the other person needs, that your love is acceptable to others." She added, "Or perhaps you weren't really gay in the first place and *that's* why you can't get worked up over what happened."

"Can I get you another drink?" The diminutive waitress addressed Stephen.

He pointed to their carafe of house red, three-quarters full. She gave it a frightened glance, then said cheerily "Right you are," and started to move away.

Stephen's forehead contracted. He called sternly, "Waitress". She turned but did not approach; her black-stockinged legs were childishly thin below a short tight skirt. He told her, "To be invited to purchase more drinks when a moment's glance would have told you we were perfectly well supplied is not service but intrusion; is not to be attended to but to be pestered."

Her doll-like face went wide-eyed with fear; then with irresponsible friendliness she came up close and said, "Oh, I know how you feel, but we've *got* to ask people if they want another drink ten minutes after their meal is served." She gave a furtive glance towards the counter and cash desk; its furtiveness would be obvious to observant management. "It's a *rule*." Her face brightened into waitress happiness and she said "Okeydokee", scurrying away.

Brenda said solemnly, "Stephen, that anger was not about *her*."

"It *is* annoying. I know places have to make a profit, but to try so blatantly to milk you for more money..."

"So you *do* mind about being exploited. Which is what Joel did to you."

Stephen laid down his knife and fork again – any old how this time, she noticed – and there was a tremor in his voice (the crust was cracking, oil was rising to the surface!) as he said, "Look, Brenda, you keep saying, suggesting, Joel was just using me, didn't, well, care for –"

"Love!"

"Well, then, love me. Look. We used to do our shopping on a Saturday morning and there was always this, well, beggar, though the word is a bit old-fashioned, but that's what he was, is, outside the Safeway. People call him Sid Safeway," – the supermarket's name, the homeliness of the nickname, the reference to something ordinary like shopping, were, on his lips, heartbreakingly incongruous with the remote impersonal abstractions of the law which were his mind's habitat: yes, there was a lot wrong with professional training that had such an unhealthy effect on a person's capacity for spontaneous thought and feeling – "a youngish man, not scruffy, really; a bit like these models, male ones I mean, you see in magazines who are sort of deliberately unkempt, unshaven.

"He, Sid Safeway, used to watch the passers-by, not aggressively, like he was trying to stare them into giving, shame them into it, but as if he wanted nothing from them, they were just people who fascinated him. If someone gave him money he kind of gave them the impression that that was incidental to why he was there, not the purpose. But he had a placard propped against him as he sat, and it read, 'I am homeless and I have not eaten for' – and a blank square of something was stuck there – 'for blank hours', and every so often he'd wipe out the figure and write in a new one. Someone brought him a hamburger from the fast food place down the road and before he touched it he changed the figure to 0. Well, Joel didn't give him money or a hamburger. He gave him a compact disc, his favourite one, the *Goldberg Variations*."

"That's *appalling*! Someone is homeless, starving, and Joel gives him some dreadful worthless symbol of, of yuppie affluence, of everything that, yes, *makes* him homeless and starving. He *mocks* him, in fact." But Stephen seemed not to hear and she saw that his eyes were lost in reminiscence: ah, he was reliving evenings when he and Joel, to that favourite, discreetly heart-tugging soundtrack, strings welling, had lived their intimate lovers' life together. She dropped indignation to offer good sense. "Well, he could have flogged it."

Stephen continued, "He separated himself from me suddenly, I had no idea he was going to do anything, and he went up to Sid Safeway and gave a funny little bow, like it was a ceremony of some kind, and presented him with the disc, the compact disc; Joel was smiling and you'd have thought he knew he was giving him the one thing he wanted in all the world and was overjoyed to be doing it. And Joel just said the one word, 'Hope', and when he rejoined me he didn't say anything about it, just said he'd get the vegetables while I got the other shopping.

"The next Saturday Sid Safeway was there as usual and Joel said to him, 'How much did you get for the CD I gave you?' and the man produced it from some pocket and said, 'I don't sell this', and Joel just turned away, as if the man didn't exist, and said to me, 'There is hope.' And his face was, well, radiant.

"I am well aware that what I have described to you would not, in the normal sense of the word, be accepted as evidence that Joel did not exploit me. Nevertheless, I have to say that it is absolutely sufficient to convince me that he did not do so." He turned his eyes to his plate and resumed his knife and fork.

Brenda gasped with compassion. She rose to her feet, all determination. "Stephen, at first you won't like what I'm going to do, but it will help you, it will break you down to where you can really make contact with your own feelings and start to really grow as a person." In a loud voice she cried "Please give me your attention everyone."

Voices went quiet, cutlery ceased to sound on plates, eyes converged on her. "This man's name is Stephen McLean. He has had a break-up in a relationship, a homosexual relationship, which is fine, being gay, I mean, but he has this problem that he's in denial about his own feelings of hurt and anger about how the other person treated him, which is very dangerous to repress. If you all know about him it will, like, help him to experience himself objectively, as he really is, and come to terms with his true feelings. Thank you." Unhurriedly she bent to pick up two plastic bags of shopping and then walked from the restaurant, imparting a conscious dignity to the large body that made her loose blouse and voluminous gathered skirt look as though they concealed several more bags. She had eaten very little of her pizza.

The silence did not break at once. Stephen's face, that had forty or fifty eyes upon it, was immobile – he might have been straining to listen to distant music – and then with complete calm he cast his eyes downwards, casually not ashamedly, and continued to eat. Slowly faces turned away, conversation resumed, glances from time to time flickered back towards him.

"I didn't order this," he said composedly. A cup of cappuccino had arrived by his plate.

The skinny little waitress, her hair close-cropped and artificially black, smiled too eagerly. "Oh, I know you didn't. It's all right. On the house. You know, after..." Her face and eyes gestured towards the door. He said, "Thank you" – politely, certainly, but exactly as though he had been dining alone and coffee had been part of his order. She backed away timidly, nodding, bright-eyed with concern, her pasty doll's face pleading with him to recognise that they were confederates with an enemy in common.

Astrid Ivask

Return Home

1. Morning

Thank God, it is dawn.
In the windows
a timid winter waking.
Soon everyone will get up.

What do you mean,
sitting there, old rag doll?
Fur cap cocked to one ear,
shod in white winter boots,
but legs too skinny to outrun,
to catch up with time.

Left behind, rag doll,
are you a watershed,
a rock in the river, do you
want to remind me of something?
Or do you tell me to let go,
as I let go of you,
of the hand
I am still holding tightly?

Only you, Mother's rag doll,
waking with me – why are you
still there? Always there,
in your corner,
a rock in dawn's flood.
A fancy cap you sport,
but you lag behind,
your legs much too weak
to keep pace with time.

2. Evening

Jagged bare branches
behind the panes
against dirty snow.
Bamboo birdcage on this side,
empty; trees also empty.
Car lights thread
through a winding artery
like blood coursing,
drop by drop.

Slow creep of illness
through your veins.

Dark red of dried blood
in a wallhanging,
splattered over a rug.

To come back to simple
childhood things,
birdcage, rag doll.

Blood courses blindly.
To feel its warmth by touch,
blood comes alive.
It is so simple,
so very little,
yet that is all there is.

Astrid Ivask

The Hardest Thing

is to find by chance –
in a book, a drawer –
one of those small
funny drawings
you used to do
to cheer me up.
To come across it as if
you had just finished
and put it there
to surprise me.

Paul Muldoon: *To Ireland, I*

Heather O'Donoghue

The most immediately striking, and, in the end, most enduringly significant point about Paul Muldoon's highly – and wonderfully – idiosyncratic book about Irish literature, *To Ireland, I*, is that it is arranged alphabetically by author. Of course, we are perfectly familiar with reference books such as dictionaries or encyclopaedias which have their entries alphabetically arranged simply for the convenience of finding any topic or word. But *To Ireland, I* is a discursive critical survey, and its alphabetical arrangement deliberately flies in the face of the usual procedures for such books, which have traditionally considered literature chronologically – to begin at the beginning – or thematically, with texts and authors grouped under broad headings such as 'The Celtic Revival' or 'The Irish Novel'. Part of Muldoon's purpose is plainly simple iconoclasm, to refuse the old ways of doing these things. And partly it's for fun, a self-set challenge that he pulls off like a clever trick. The joke is even funnier when Muldoon wriggles on his own hook, such as when he reaches the letter F before the point he wants to make about the poet Samuel Ferguson, so he must instruct the reader "I'm not going to comment extensively on [him] just now, but I do assure you that I have a purpose, and will return to [him] later". I most enjoyed Muldoon's wry postscript to the U entry (James Ussher, 1581-1656): "If you're wondering what I'm going to do when I get to X, so am I".

But the serious purpose behind the alphabetical arrangement informs the whole basis of this book. The alphabet is a conventional ordering system which, as a reviewer of the *Oxford English Dictionary* once put it "simultaneously decontextualizes and recontextualizes the entries". In other words, all the old connections between writers – that one followed another in history, or that one wrote the same kind of poem as another – are ignored by alphabetical arrangement, and new connections are constructed. This is in fact a classically post-modernist thing to do. But the new connections which Muldoon is constructing amount to a radical new look at what constitutes his whole subject – Irish literature. Muldoon is saying that it really doesn't matter what order you consider these authors in. What links them is not time, place or language, but Irishness. So what exactly is Irish about Irish literature? This is not a question explicitly asked by Muldoon, but *To Ireland, I* (ironically enough subtitled *The Clarendon Lectures in English Literature 1998*) is nothing less than an attempt at answering this most difficult of questions.

Heather O'Donoghue

English Literature may be paraphrased and redefined as 'Literature written in English', but that won't, of course, work with Irish literature. The long history of Ireland's status as a British colony means that the nationality of Irish authors in earlier centuries is endlessly problematic – and continues, to a lesser degree, to be so, especially for British anthologists: look at Seamus Heaney's understandable objections to being classed as a British poet. And finally, a further complication: two of the greatest Irish authors, Beckett and Joyce, wrote from outside Ireland, and produced some of their work in neither Irish nor English. All this is not to mention the celebrated euphemism of 'the two traditions' in Ireland. Muldoon's answer, which informs every page of *To Ireland, I*, is both inclusive enough to account for the extraordinary variety of Irishness, and exclusive enough to make sense of the variety. Irish authors, this book demonstrates, refer constantly to one another in their work. Muldoon sees this dense web of intertextuality as a sort of 'ceo sidhe' enveloping Irish literature, and the links are at the level of individual words (both Irish and English – and sometimes French) and repeated motifs, or story patterns. Like the alphabet, these textual links transcend language, culture, chronology and place; alphabetically and intertextually, Samuel Beckett comes next to Elizabeth Bowen.

It's typical of Muldoon's playful and provocative writing that his great project to undermine by alphabetical arrangement the old ways of writing about Irish literature begins with an undermining of his own procedure, for the first author he considers is also the earliest: Amergin, whose name means 'wonder-birth'. This is the first coincidence in a book which rejoices in linguistic coincidences of all kinds. What is more, the poem attributed to Amergin in the *Lebor Gabála Érenn* exhibits the qualities which Muldoon goes on to claim as defining characteristics of Irishness: he speaks 'for Erin', and he speaks from a liminal place – from, as his 'Alphabet Calendar of Amergin' puts it, "the unhewn dolmen arch", the threshold of two worlds. Muldoon's own title, *To Ireland, I*, (spoken by King Duncan's son Donalbain, in *Macbeth*, as he and his brother discuss their exile) itself displays this liminality: not in Ireland, and not out of it, but a place in thought, in intention, in between.

The best way to demonstrate Muldoon's critical method – the way he establishes verbal and thematic links between Irish authors – is simply to illustrate a couple of examples of it: first, an example of verbal intertextuality, and second, of reworked themes.

Alphabetically, 'Anonymous' precedes 'Beckett'. Muldoon's fourth anonymous poem is a ninth-century May-day poem, in Irish. Four short lines describe pollen-laden bees: "Berait beich/(becc a nert)/bert bond,/bochtai blaíth" (Bees of small strength carry bundles of culled blossom on their feet). Samuel Beckett, Muldoon argues "would surely have delighted in" the juxtaposition of the word for bees, 'beich', and the adjective for small, 'becc', not only because both echo the sound of the first syllable of his own name, but because 'beich', Muldoon claims, is cognate with 'bac' which means, according to Dinneen, any number of different pointy things. 'The Blackbird over Belfast Lough', in Gerard Murphy's *Early Irish Lyrics*, opens with the line "Int en bec", referring to the blackbird's yellow beak, and this brings us dramatically round to the French 'bec', not only beak, but also the nib of a pen. Since, as Muldoon rather carefully puts it, the word "may be construed as a version of" the Old English word 'bec', a beech tree, which in turn 'lies behind' the word for 'book', then Muldoon's triumphant conclusion that the first syllable of Beckett's name is "both pen and paper". Etymologists will no doubt be infuriated by all this. But wait. Muldoon refers us to the passage in Beckett's *Malone Dies* in which Mr Saposcat buys (from himself) a fountain pen for his son, a present on the day of his son's examination. The nib of the pen is particularly drawn attention to, because Mr Saposcat's wife suggests that the boy may need to get used to the nib before his exam – or even change it. But the pen must be left in the box. And what is pictured on the box? "A bird, its yellow beak agape to show it was singing". What is at issue here is not Beckett's knowledge of, or allusion to, Old Irish poetry, his 'Gaelic underpinning', though plainly Muldoon is emphasizing an 'Irish' connection here, but whether Beckett's juxtaposition of the nib of the pen and the beak of the blackbird is simply coincidence, or whether all that etymological rigmarole in some mysterious way does reflect Beckett's creative thought processes. The title *Krapp's Last Tape* (and the outrageous double meaning of its French equivalent) comes in for similar analysis.

On the level of literary motifs, Muldoon has an abiding concern with later re-workings of the Old Irish 'feth fíadha', the magic mist which marks the boundary between this world and another, a liminal place and time at which certain individuals may pass from one to the other.

According to Muldoon, this passage often takes place during a hunt with hounds (the fairy folk appearing sometimes as deer, or other animals) to the ringing of bells or unearthly music. So if you're at all persuaded by Muldoon's exposition of Beckett's 'Gaelic underpinning', you'll recognise at once a version of the 'feth fíadha' in *Krapp's Last Tape*, as Krapp imagines that he might "be again on Croghan on a Sunday morning, in the haze, with the bitch, stop and listen to the bells". But Beckett is followed by Bowen, and a version of the 'feth fíadha' in her work is an altogether more surprising proposition. And yet, in her extraordinarily chilling short story, 'The Demon Lover', Elizabeth Bowen describes how Mrs Dover, returning to her empty London home evacuated during the Second World War, experiences a sudden panic attack, rushing out into the street and escaping – she supposes – by taxi. As Muldoon shows us, the taxi "presented its black rump" to her, and she "panted up from behind" just as the clock strikes seven. The story ends with Mrs Dover's screams as the taxi accelerates and she recognizes the driver. One doesn't need to recall the story's title to understand what is happening here, or to recognize the appropriateness of Muldoon's identification of a 'feth fíadha' motif.

Similarly, while one might be irritated by Muldoon's play on names, C.S. *Lew*is, his heroine *Lu*cy, the Celtic studies academic R.S. *Lo*omis and the god *Lu*gh, nonetheless, in the opening of *The Lion, the Witch and the Wardrobe* (in which the wardrobe itself is just the kind of liminal threshold between two worlds which Muldoon calls a narthex) Lucy hears an unexplained noise, is enveloped in the fur coats hanging in the wardrobe, and passes through to another realm in which her guide is Faun – the deer of the 'feth fíadha'. The important thing here is that Bowen and Lewis are unequivocally incorporated into the Irish tradition, the one a member of the Anglo-Irish ascendancy, and the other forever associated more with Oxford than with the Belfast in which he was born. The old connections of time, place and culture, which would separate such authors as Bowen and Lewis off from Gaelic tradition, are transcended.

If we regard alphabetical arrangement as a means of disrupting these old connections, as a sort of disordering of chronological and thematic groupings in favour of random juxtapositions, then it may be appropriate to refer here to Chaos theory, a set of mathematical ideas that tries to make sense out of the apparently random, disordered patterns which occur spontaneously in nature, such as the irregular outline of the coast, or a leaf. When these apparently random patterns are plotted out in a diagram, it emerges that for all their unpredictable movement, certain points are, mysteriously, repeatedly recrossed and returned to. Mathematicians call these focal points 'strange attractors', and if we can regard Muldoon's succession of alphabetically arranged authors as a series of unpredictable juxtapositions, then their strange attractor, which Muldoon's analysis repeatedly swoops away from and endlessly loops back to, is undoubtedly James Joyce's short story 'The Dead'.

According to conventional readings, the dead of the title are the ghosts of the characters' own pasts, recalled by those characters at the party in the Miss Morkans' house, and after, by Gretta Conroy, in the Gresham Hotel, where she and her husband Gabriel stay after the party. As Muldoon reads the story, the characters themselves are 'the dead' – shades of the archetypal figures from Old Irish legend, or their more recent Celtic revivalist transmitters to the English language tradition. Thus, the Miss Morkans' house (the name may be a deliberate echo of the Morrigan, given all the crow imagery in the text) relates to the feasting hall of Da Derga in the Old Irish story *Togail Bruidne Da Derga*, and Gabriel Conroy's name, especially as pronounced by Lily the caretaker's daughter, with three syllables, identifies him with King Conaire Mór himself. Uncontroversially, Muldoon alludes to the resonance in so much Irish literature of how Gabriel Conroy's spiritual awakening is symbolised – "The time had come for him to set out on his journey westward" – but more daringly relates the animal imagery which infuses Gabriel's thoughts about Gretta in the Gresham to the symbolic marriage of Old Irish kings to their kingdom with the ritual involving a mare, as described by Giraldus Cambrensis.

If this sort of analysis raises an embarrassed snigger, I don't believe Muldoon would feel aggrieved or undermined by that. He constantly treads a fine line between the serious and the jokey, brilliantly exploiting the embarrassment of uncertainty. Can the nutmeg on the Miss Morkans' custards really be meant to recall Sir Alfred Nutt, the nineteenth century Celticist who wrote the notes to Kuno Meyer's edition of the *Imram Brain*? Or is that a self-parodying joke, as Muldoon seems half to concede as he wonders whether we readers will think the suggestion "totally nuts"? Is the reference to Michael Furey's employment in the gasworks a solemn bit of social placing of the character on Joyce's part, or a play on 'geas-works', recalling Old Irish geasa, or taboos? And just as we try to work out whether to take this suggestion seriously or not, Muldoon raises the teasing possibility that the whole thing may be no more than a bit of *guess*work.

Heather O'Donoghue

As one might expect, Muldoon finds echoes of 'The Dead' in the work of a number of other Irish writers, but his stress on Joyce's predecessors, those significant feeder springs into the great reservoir of 'The Dead'. There's an odd contrast, however, between the way in which Muldoon's excavation (or, indeed, creation) of Old Irish echoes in 'The Dead' seems to demean the serious intent of the story, and the unmistakable reverence with which Muldoon regards Joyce's work: "One could be forgiven for thinking that all Irish, and indeed, almost all of world literature had been produced merely as a 'reamh sceal', a prelude or preliminary piece to the work of the greatest of all Irish writers, James Joyce." There are those who see 'The Dead' as effortlessly embodying the big political questions hanging over Ireland: Gabriel's rejection of Irish as 'his' language; the genial exchanges with Mr Browne, politely described as being "of the other persuasion". Others admire the delicacy and insight with which Joyce portrays Gabriel's sexually-charged anticipation of his and his wife's stay at the Gresham (Muldoon strangely describes the decision to spend the night away from home and their children as "strange"). The poignant evocation of past nostalgia may be felt to be enough in itself to carry the story. All such readers will be at best sceptical of Muldoon's minute etymological analysis of Miss Ivor's name, or the significance of her brooch, or un-low-cut bodice. And yet such scepticism fails to take into account the other major defining characteristic which Muldoon sees in Irish literature: the hidden meanings; the dualities inherent in words and phrases; the gap between appearance and reality in a text which Muldoon punningly labels "Eriny" and which of course, his own work most manifestly exemplifies.

One might want to argue that even if Muldoon can 'read in' to a text all these allusions, double meanings and etymological references, it is still far from clear that authors wrote their texts in anticipation that they would be subjected to such ingenious analysis – in other words, did not *mean* all this wordplay. The exception, of course, is Joyce's *Finnegan's Wake*, and Muldoon's critical practice is ideally suited to this text. No one could take exception to, or fail to enjoy and admire Muldoon's exposition of the single phrase with which Joyce apparently refers to himself: "no espellor mor so" – all the more since Joyce's own linguistic inventiveness gives carte blanche to Muldoon's critical inventiveness. According to Muldoon's reading, 'mor' is the English 'more' without an 'e', but also the Irish 'mór': 'big', and the 'so' a version of Joyce's name in Irish, Seoighe: the whole might mean 'Great Joyce'. 'No' means 'or' in Irish; 'espellor' combines ideas of spells, or magic charms, with 'gospeller' – both indicating the power of speech – and also the Irish word for antlers, which might refer to the cuckoldry at the heart of 'usyless *Ulysses*', or even the deer of the 'feth fíadha'. Finally, Muldoon relates the Irish word 'speal' to 'spelt' (wheat) and therefore spalpeen. Thus, Muldoon argues, Joyce is associating himself with "itinerant day-labourers from the west of Ireland, who worked for almost no return" – an association "at once touching and true".

Perhaps no other text could bear this kind of analysis (though I was rather taken by Muldoon's musings on Swift's naming of his hero Gulliver, the first syllable echoing the 'gall' of the Irish word for foreigner, and the second two a version of 'Eber', the name at the heart of Hibernia and, in another sudden swoop back to 'The Dead', Miss *Ivors*.) It is certainly disconcerting to come across a kind of literary criticism which makes no clear distinction between scholarly fact and subjective speculation – and which indeed deliberately blurs the line between the two. Muldoon's overarching, if implicit, project, to define the Irishness in Irish literature, depends on his detailed setting out of a vast number of intertextual references and verbal echoes. The obvious question is, does Muldoon discover the connections, or is he inventing them? The only possible answer is, that it really doesn't matter.

John Wakeman

Trappings

The house subsides, its levels telling lies;
one step might land you on the mantelpiece.
Paper peels from plaster, plaster from lathe.
You can see the wires inside like plaited hair
or knitted nerves gnawed ragged by the mice.
Some rooms are dangerous; your little suite
is boarded up for good, the windows blinded.

One foolish night in spring I took the fancy
to march again by moonlight in the playroom –
'Lillibullero' on the gramophone, the tasselled drum.
Mostly I sit here in the library
with both bars blazing and the gin to hand,
turning the pages back, scanning the margins.
Stories, it used to be. Now only history.

The other day some youth knocked on the door.
He said this place had once been where he lived –
spoke of the traps he set for rabbits in the covert,
that cross-eyed Cupid by the summerhouse,
his boat of skins, the lake's profundity.
I sent him packing. Now I wonder.

A Siberian Notebook

Theo Dorgan has said that living and writing in Cork was like "being in Siberia"

Words freeze as they form,
icicles hang from them, brittle
beauty poised on the point
of meaning – ice on the tongues
of those who've braved the cold,
elaborate patterns delicately moulded.

Accents would rise and fall
if allowed, if anyone would listen.
Stories would criss-cross the Lee,
slip into the back-streets
by the Cathedral to have a smoke
and guffaw at the bawdy jokes

bandied between the linen
on the lines. Poets might once
have rhymed sailors as retailers,
plundered epic narratives from
the mix of words freely
scattered on the quay.

But numb winters have rolled
down from the north, and ideas
are cut off from the outside world.
The city is wrapped up in itself, lining
the inside of frayed overcoats
with fragments of novels, unsung ballads

to keep out the splinters of wind.
Many now are hidden underground,
working to preserve their livelihood
caught up in some strange subversive

world where a storyteller's tales
are preserved in bags of salt.

The rebel voice will always come
in from the cold, a defiant name
etched in breath upon a windowpane.

Frost

I try to make a difference,
press my lips to the world

let my breath brush the leaves
of grass, still the troubled

murmuring of water, the chill
in early morning movement.

Understand me when I say
you must not mourn my absence;

savour the lustre in the land,
the richness when I'm gone.

Michael Hartnett and the Gaelic Muse

Gabriel Fitzmaurice

"Poetry is what is lost in translation." There are certain critics who believe that poetry cannot be translated from one language to another. There are certain poets who do not wish their poetry to be translated. Why, then, is poetry translated?

To take the Irish language as an instance, it is sometimes said that it is an act of cultural imperialism to translate it into English. There are certain poets and critics who object to such translation as a matter of principle. Why, then, would a poet bother to translate from the Irish?

Michael Hartnett, my sometime advisor, my friend forever, translated (from the Irish, Spanish, Hungarian, Chinese and German) because he loved, and sympathised with, certain poets and poems. He was enthralled by, and in thrall to, the Irish language.

He moved away from English in 1975 when he published *A Farewell to English* until 1985 when he published his *Inchicore Haiku*; he moved to Templeglantine in West Limerick, a place he deemed to be a "breac Ghaeltacht", a place where the Irish language still lingered. He had a vision. A kind of 'aisling', in the sense that the Gaelic poets of the seventeenth and eighteenth centuries had, a fond hope that a Gaelic order would again prevail. Alas, no ethereal beauty (no 'aisling') appeared to him out of the skies. He had barely settled in his 'breac Ghaeltacht' when he heard an old man walking the road singing – in Irish, Michael fondly hoped: there was 'sean-nós' (the old style of singing in Irish) in his voice. But when the old man came nearer, Michael could hear, to his mixed disappointment and amusement, that he was singing 'Yes We Have No Bananas', a popular song of yesteryear. The 'aisling' vanished. (She had never appeared in the first place). The vision remained.

Michael wrote almost exclusively in Irish from 1975 to 1985, though he did write the occasional poem in English during that period – a poem, for instance, on the death on hunger strike of Bobby Sands ('Who killed Bobby Sands?' modelled on the nursery rhyme 'Who killed Cock Robin?') which he submitted to *The Irish Times*, but which was rejected on political grounds though it wasn't a poem in support of the Provisional IRA; and 'Maiden Street Ballad', a lovesong to the street of his childhood which was published in his native Newcastle West in 1981. Ostensibly, the poet Hartnett was dismissive of these poems. But, privately, he was well pleased with them. They weren't poetry but ballads, he used to say. In his Preface to the 'Maiden Street Ballad' he asks: "What is the difference between a ballad and a poem?" And he answers: "Well a ballad can often contain poetry – all the best ones do – but a poem must depend on an inner emotion and not on narrative, geography or history – it must not have a programme as the ballad does". He goes on to tell us that he "used the metre of 'The Limerick Rake', the best Hiberno-English ballad ever written in this county". "I have not hesitated," he informs us, "to use all the coventions of such a song. In this way I have been able to purge from my system the folk-images and rhythms that all my reading in modern literature could not eradicate (not that they could not be used to create a 'modern' work: but I simply don't wish to use them."

This is the reason, I believe, that he translates seventeenth and eighteenth century poets like Dáibhí Ó Bruadair and Aogán Ó Rathaille – it offers him an opportunity to make poems in the old mould that are at the same time contemporary works of art. Another aspect of the poet.

Of course there is poetry in the English ballads he wrote after he had said his farewell to English, the language he felt was "a necessary sin/the perfect language to sell pigs in". And Michael knew well that 'Who Killed Bobby Sands?' and 'Maiden Street Ballad' contained poetry. But they were "bastards". He concealed them among his community, his people around Newcastle West. Five years after he composed his 'Maiden Street Ballad' he wrote:

> My English dam bursts
> and out stroll all my bastards.
> Irish shakes its head

and he published his *Inchicore Haiku*, a sequence of eighty-seven haiku celebrating his move to Inchicore in Dublin. Bidding farewell to Maiden Street, he says of the people of Inchicore:

> My dead father shouts
> from his eternal Labour:
> 'These are your people'.

Writing in English again. Between 1975 and 1985, between his *A Farewell to English* and his *Inchicore Haiku*, much had happened to trouble the poet – his father died, his marriage broke up, he left his 'breac Ghaeltacht' and moved back to Dublin (which he had left in 1975 for Templeglantine), and he was drinking heavily. From then on he would publish in Irish and English.

While he was domiciled in Templeglantine, he would regularly summon me to meet him (in the Devon Inn in 'Glantine, more often in his favourite pubs in Newcastle West, very occasionally in the family home in the townland of Glandarragh, just outside Templeglantine). He needed to talk. About poetry. About what he was writing. About the Irish language. About translation. When it came to translation, he believed that the translator (i.e. he himself) should be faithful to the original text. But he was a poet. It was poetry he made when he translated. Sure, there were given things, the thought of the original poem, its language, text and context, its rhythm and music; but Hartnett the translator understood that it was his duty as a poet to make a new poem. A version that would be sympathetic, a poem re-created.

This is what he has achieved in *Ó Rathaille*, his translations of Aogán Ó Rathaille (c. 1675–1729), "perhaps", according to the *An Duanaire: Poems of the Dispossessed* of Seán Ó Tuama and Thomas Kinsella, "the greatest of Irish poets, writing in Irish or English, between the seventeenth century and the twentieth". Within a year of the publication of *Ó Rathaille*, Michael Hartnett died, of liver failure, in a Dublin hospital.

Certain critics have demonstrated that there are flaws, mainly minor inaccuracies, in these translations. But no seer is without flaw. Looking at the larger picture, Hartnett has done well. Very well. Ó Rathaille lives in Hartnett's translations – Hartnett has revitalised him, giving him a fresh voice, a musical, rhythmical, colloquial voice, a voice for today. If, at times, Hartnett comes too close to the 'sráid éigse' (low poetry) that he, and the high Gaelic poets of an earlier age, condemned (for instance he gives us "she'll barren become and lie with none till back comes Mac an Cheannaí" for "'s go mbeidh sí 'na spreas gan luí le fear/go bhfillfidh Mac an Cheannaí"), let us forgive him. This was a calculated risk he took. This is Hartnett taking on another aspect. This is a homage to the Irish language, and his poem-freedom, freedom from his self-imposed refusal to "create a 'modern' work...[using] all the conventions of...song" – song like 'The Limerick Rake' out of which he made the 'Maiden Street Ballad'.

Gabriel Fitzmaurice

Behind Hartnett there is always Ó hAirtnéide, his alter ego. The English language and the Irish. The translator (Hartnett, he calls him) comes between the two languages. In translating, between two languages, he finds a place where he can be true to the music and the song metres (the 'sráid éigse'!) he cannot accomodate in his mainstream poetry. And he revels in it. As Michael Coady, a fellow Munster poet, put it in his poem 'Solo':

> Now's the time –
> with the dance still on
> and the band swinging –
>
> to stand up
> and blow
> ad lib
> with all the wrong notes
> you dare.

Hartnett/Ó hAirtnéide has earned that freedom.

In the end, Hartnett has given us Ó Rathaille's range and his rage, his 'aisling' poems, his elegies, his political poems, his satires, his poems to his one time patrons before the collapse of the Gaelic order humbled both poet and patron, and, lastly, his poems of destitution. In doing so, he has redeemed Ó Rathaille for me, he has aroused my sympathy for the haughty poets who fell on hard times.

Michael Hartnett
His early days in Newcastle West: 1941 – 1961
John Cussen

> We were such golden children, never to be dust
> Singing in the street alive and loud

The recent death of the poet Michael Hartnett is a reminder of his formative years growing up in Newcastle West in the 1940s and 50s. His published autobiographical writings are fugitive and scattered but through his poems we can piece together an evocative mosaic of the town and the times. Michael was born in 1941 the eldest son of Denis Hartnett and Bridget Hartnett (née Halpin). The biographical notes in his books have been bedevilled by the factual information that he was born in Croom and the assumption therefore that his family were living in Croom. This is of course quite incorrect. He was born in Croom for the very good reason that the hospital there had then a maternity unit attached. His parents at that time were living in Connolly's Terrace, later moving to Church Street and Maiden Street. Michael's grandfather E.P.H. (Ned Harnett or Hartnett) was a tailor in North Quay. He came to Newcastle from Athea in the 1870s. A thesis could be written about the distinction between the spelling of the surname and whether it should be Harnett or Hartnett. Suffice to say that Harnett is considered more genteel and Michael himself settled for Hartnett.

Michael's 'Maiden Street Ballad' paints a vivid picture of his youth in Maiden Street:

> Behind Nash's garage we played pitch and toss
> or sat on the footpath the tinkers to watch
>
> as they walloped each other because of a horse
>   outside Bill Flynn's pub of an evening.
> Oh gone are the days of our simple past-times
> When rawking an orchard was the worst of our crimes:
> We fought with our fists and we never used knives
>   And ran like the hare when the priest came.
>
> We played marbles and skellit, and blue with the cold

> We started up bonfires right out in the road:
> We had negotiable comics and our chanies were gold
>> And marble sweets were twelve a penny.
> We cracked nuts in the autumn, caught collies in crocks
> And hunted for crawfish at the back of the Docks:
> We ducked into Latchfords, myself and Mike Fox
>> And ate Peggy's Leg for our dinner.

Michael went to the Convent school and then on to the Courtenay Boys' School. He seems to have happy memories of the Courtenay School where his bright intelligence was recognised by the headmaster, Frank Finucane, who also encouraged his first efforts at writing poetry. He wasn't so complimentary about the old schoolhouse itself, however, describing it as "unbelievable". In the summer the swallows built in the large beams inside the rooms, flying in and out all day to feed their young. One of my favourite pastimes was drowning woodlice in the inkwells, as they all fell in ridiculous numbers from the rafters!

Michael graduated to The Library, Jim Breen's secondary school in 1956. He recollects his English teacher there with his sarcastic comment "meditating the Muse, Hartnett?" when caught daydreaming.

He writes some hard things in his recollection of Newcastle West at that time and its claustrophobia, "its rich and poor, its bullying priest, the reading of the dues from the pulpit, the quashed scandals, the mass emigration of the young". He recognised, however, that the town and the countryside in many ways had made him, "the mountains are miniature, the woods are copses at best, but it is soft, beautiful inland country, very green and overlush in the summer."

Michael regularly escaped from the town to stay with his grandmother Bridget Halpin who lived on a small farm in the townland of Camas. He has written beautifully about her and she obviously had a great influence on him.

> She was a summer dance at the crossroads.
> She was a card game where a nose was broken.
> She was a song that nobody sings
> he was a house ransacked by soldiers.

She was a language seldom spoken.
She was a child's purse, full of useless things.

Michael first shook the dust of Newcastle West from his shoes in 1961 when he took a one way ticket to London. As he said himself, "An air of hope and sadness always hung over the local railway station. I myself, complete with cardboard suitcase took a single ticket to Euston in 1961." He would be back of course, but that is another story. His hometown permeates his poetry and his hometown is proud of him.

> But now what can I say of a small country town
> That is not like Killarney, known all the world round?
> That has not for beauty won fame or renown
>   But still all the same is quite charming?
> I have seen some fine cities in my traveller's quest,
> Put Boston and London and Rome to the test
> But I wouldn't give one foot of Newcastle West
>   For all of their beauty and glamour.

Manna in the Morning: Remembering Francis Stuart

Eugene O'Connell

Madeleine Meissner was a twenty-four year old student at Berlin University when she first noticed the lean new English lecturer Francis Stuart "dressed in flannel trousers and dark blue pullover", more like a fisherman than a professor.An émigré herself from the Kashubian district near Danzig in the disputed German/Polish corridor region, she instinctively fell for her new teacher who introduced her to the Irish literary world in his 'Essay' and 'Conversational' classes.Francis Stuart had published eleven novels by 1939, including the acclaimed 1932 books *Pigeon Irish* and *The Coloured Dome*. *We have Kept the Faith* was a first collection of poems published in 1923, the year after his release from Portlaoise and Tintown prisons, where he had served a year for his pro-Republican activities during the Irish Civil War. He married Iseult Gonne in 1923 but the marriage had failed by 1939 when he went to work in Berlin. Francis' other job was to broadcast a weekly message to Ireland for German radio. These talks were pro-Republican and reflected De Valera's quaint ideal of "our own life on our own soil, free from the tyranny of money". Incredibly, the head of the station, Dr Hartmann, broadcast in the Irish language to Ireland.

Madeleine remembers another Irishman, William Joyce – 'Lord Haw Haw', who gained cult status for his vitriolic anti-British propaganda, and was later executed by them, with great affection "he was always in high spirits, bristled with energy and brought a whiff of life into the office, where he was popular with everybody." In her memoir *Manna in the Morning*, Madeleine, later to become Francis' second wife for more than fifty years, remembers the ration cards and the normality of the early war years and the intensity of her effort to build an inner Jerusalem, a sanctum, which the lovers could retreat to when the harsh realities of the war started kicking in.

After a brief surreal period in 1943 when the radio station moved to Luxembourg, where Francis continued his broadcasts and they drank pink champagne with every meal in "that most bourgeois of countries", the couple returned to Berlin where the fierce bombing raids of the next two years had begun. On the morning after their flat was shattered by a blast Madeleine was to write "and that is how my first prayer was born in me because prayer was then and is still for me the intensity of living. How strange and miraculous it seems to me that my soul started to live while the

city around me was dying, I learned in those days what prayer was all about..."
Incredibly, they still sunbathed on roofs between air-raids and she sat for exams that
took place in cellars, and dreamed of another life where "Fear had gone, love had
become my vocation".

By the scorching summer of 1944 the city had begun to resemble a moonscape piled
with rubble that even the forced labour imported from the east was failing to clear.
It was the summer too that Francis nursed his old friend Frank Ryan, the famous
Republican who led the International Brigade in the Spanish Civil War. Madeleine
and Francis were two of the twelve people who attended the funeral of the great
socialist figure of the 30s when he was buried at Loschwitz Cemetery. By the tenth
of May 1944, the university was hit and with news of the Red Army's advance from
the east, the Stuarts left Berlin for Munich; they had become refugees. Not for the
first time, Madeleine could empathise with the 'Wandering Jews' of the Old
Testament, "And all the time the Lord went before them, by day a pillar of cloud
to guide them on their journey, by night a pillar of fire to give them light, so that
they could travel night and day." Food was a constant preoccupation during the
winter of 1944 in Munich when the city was firebombed under the command of
Arthur 'Bomber' Harris to test the morale of the civilian population and their
loyalty to the Nazi regime.

There were walks in the 'Englische Garten' and study in the library where they read
Mr's Eckhardt and Rilke, and of course the psalms, "The worse outward life
became, the more we had the need to build our own Jerusalem". In the spring of
1945 they left Munich to head south, boarding train after train and receiving little
welcome from the native Bavarians – a province saturated with refugees. Francis had
a narrow escape near Lake Constance on the border with Switzerland when he
stumbled on a retreating German regiment, luckily their officer recognised his Irish
passport and told him that the Republican Ernie O'Malley, who wrote *On Another
Man's Wound* was one of his heroes.

Stuart's nationality prevented him from entering Switzerland where they waited
weeks at the border until finally on the second of May 1945 France occupied Bavaria
and the war was over for them. On November of that year they were arrested and
put into Oberstadt Prison in Bregenz where Madeleine was accused of spying; a
ploy she has always maintained, by the British to get at Francis because of his war-

time broadcasts. They spent Christmas of 1945 in prison where she realised at last the truth of the psalm that she would have to find the 'Promised Land' within herself and not in any earthly Eden, "He hath put a new song in my mouth; yea thy law O Lord is within my heart". Francis was transported to Germany on the twenty-fourth of May 1946 and expected to be transported to the English Zone where he would face trial and possible execution, but on July the thirteenth – the day before Bastille Day – he was freed. They went to live in Frieburg where Madeleine gave English lessons to East European refugees hoping to go to the promised land of America, and Francis continued his writing.

In August 1949, Madeleine arrived in Paris to be greeted by Francis who had travelled there some weeks earlier with a bunch of white carnations. His two novels, *The Pillar of Cloud* and *Redemption* had been published by Victor Gollanz to the wide acclaim of critics like Compton McKenzie who wrote, "I think *Redemption* is a magnificent book and if its beauty and terror do not win Francis Stuart the recognition he deserves I shall despair of contemporary criticism". They renewed friendship with Stuart's old friend Liam O'Flaherty, the novelist and short story writer, "who opened a suitcase full of wonderful tales, drank a lot" and shared a love of horse racing with Francis Stuart. They moved to London in 1951 and married on the twenty-eighth of April, just five weeks after the death of Iseult Gonne. They came to live in Ireland in 1957 in a cottage in The Reask in Dunsaughlin, Co. Meath where Francis wrote many books but Madeleine only one, *Manna in the Morning* which she ends with the words:

> Many years ago when I was in pain and suffering I turned to the Bible to the psalms and great literature. It came quite easily and instinctively to me. I lived in those days a very intense life. What I find much harder now is to keep that intensity of long ago alive and not lose sight of the vision I had then. I had grasped in times of stress that there is no comfort except in God but when I plunged into everyday life that message got blurred. I was not so foolish as to think that I could find fulfilment in earthly pleasures but I thought that my love could stand out like a rock against all pitfalls. Gradually it dawned on me that my love is far from perfect. It is indeed very self-seeking. I had to learn that the gift of love consists of fighting our own selfish greedy possessive ego.

I am lucky that in those dark hours I was given the power to mend it time and time again, but it was not I who did the actual healing, it was a kind of grace that pulled me out of the pit and put me on the road again, the heart a bit battered but intact nonetheless...

Notes on contributors

Barbara Brown is Emeritus Professor of English and Anglo-Irish Literatures at the University of West Virginia, Marshall Campus, in Huntington, WV. In 1994 she moved to Dublin.

Paul Brownsey trained as a journalist on leaving school. He left journalism to go to university, and is now a lecturer in philosophy at Glasgow University. His stories have appeared in a variety of publications, mainly Scottish, though he was a prizewinner in the Co. Clare-based Nora Fahy Literary Awards in 1997 and was published in New Series: *Departures*, Vol 2.

Anne Comerford has twice been awarded first place in the Scottish International Open Poetry Competition and has been honoured in both the Hopkins and Syllables competitions. In 1999, she won the Boyle Arts Festival Poetry Competition. Her work has been published in many anthologies and she gives readings at various venues in the south-east.

Tommy Curran, native of Dublin, has lived in Cork since 1988. He makes a living as a DO IT ALL HIMSELF (smalltime) builder. Art, of the literary kind, is the love of his life. He has had work published in Ireland, England, the USA and Australia.

John Cussen works as a solicitor in Newcastle West. He is also a well-known local historian and contributes articles to the *Limerick Leader*. He was a longtime friend of Michael Hartnett.

Anne Dean was born in Tipperary and now lives in Dublin. Her poetry has been published in anthologies and journals including *Poetry Ireland Review*, *Cuirt Journal* and *Books Ireland*. She has won many prizes for her poetry including recently, the Cathal Bui Competition and the Golden Pen Competition.

Dympna Dreyer, a retired schoolteacher from Tipperary, was last year's winner of the *Cork Literary Review*. Her poetry has been published in magazines such as, *Poetry Ireland Review*, *Edgeworth*, *Stroan* and *Women's Works*. She has won numerous prizes for poetry including being a finalist in the Scottish International

Open Poetry Competition in 1998. Her first collection of poetry, *Come Sun, Come Snow*, is due out at the end of this year.

Gabriel Fitzmaurice is a poet and editor who works as a primary school teacher in Moyvane, Co. Kerry. His most recent work includes: *Kerry on my Mind* and an anthology of poetry for children, *Rusty Nails and Astronauts*. A new collection of his poetry will be published shortly.

Matthew Geden is one of our most promising young poets. He has been widely published and read recently at the Dublin Writers' Centre.

Maurice Harmon is Emeritus Professor of Anglo-Irish Literature at University College Dublin. His poetry has been published in *Poetry Ireland Review*, *Cyphers*, *Stet*, *Irish University Review*, *London Magazine*, *The Tablet* and *The Honest Ulsterman*. He has had two collections published by Three Spires: *The Book of Precedance* and *Stillness at Kiawah*, and has a collection forthcoming from Salmon Press.

Donal Horgan was born in Killarney and now works as a school teacher in Cork City. He is a playwright and historian who has previously been published in the *Cork Literary Review* Vols 5 and 6. His most recent works are *The Rise and Fall of Enver Hodska* and *Echo after Echo*, a history of Killarney.

Astrid Ivask, a native of Latvia, spent most of her life in the United States, only moving to Ireland in 1991. She has published seven collections of poetry in Latvian and two in English, including *At the Fallow's Edge* and *Oklahoma Poems*. She has received several awards for her poetry, poetic prose and writing for children and her work has been translated and anthologised in a dozen languages. She is also an active essayist and translator.

Kevin Kiely works as New Writing Editor of *Books Ireland*. His poetry has been widely published including *Poetry Ireland Review*, *Anvil*, *Criterion*, *Edinburgh Review*, *Foolscap* (London), *The Literary Review* (NJ), and *Chapman* (Scotland). His play *Multiple Indiscretions* was broadcast on RTE Radio in 1997. His most recent novel *Mere Mortals* was published by Poolbeg in 1989. He is currently working on *The Authorised Biography of Francis Stuart*.

Noel King is a native of Co. Kerry. His haiku, poetry, short stories, articles and reviews have appeared in many productions at home and abroad. He is also the editor of *Podium*, the Kerry Arts Review.

Chuck Kruger was born in Finger Lakes, New York in 1938, where he spent his time "traipsing around old Iroquois hunting and burial grounds and hearing stories". He worked for twenty-six years as a secondary school teacher in Switzerland and moved to Ireland in 1992. His work has been extensively published and broadcast in Ireland, the USA, the UK and Switzerland. A poet and a novelist, his most recent published works include: *Birdsong, Butterflies and Bees* and *The Man who Talks to Himself;* next in line is his soon to be published collection of short stories: *Flotsam and Jetsam.*

Brian Mackey was born in England but grew up Kerry. He has been extensively published in poetry magazines in the UK, Canada and Australia, as well as Irish publications such as *Poetry Ireland Review*, *The Honest Ulsterman*, and most recently in *The Shop*. A retired doctor, he now runs a bookshop in Schull.

Niall MacMonagle was born in Killarney in 1954. He teaches in Wesley College Dublin and has edited: the *Lifelines* anthologies, *Real Cool*, *Outside and In*, *Poetry Now* and *Slow Time.*

Giovanni Malito is a poet and scientist. Some of the tanka reproduced in these pages have appeared in *Raw Nerv2*, *American Tanka*, and *Time Haiku*. Soon to be published works include: *To be the Fourth Wise Man* (Own World, US 2000) and *Notes of a Physics Teacher* (OHT Press, US 2000).

Nigel McLoughlin was born in Enniskillen and now lives in Co. Donegal. He has been published widely in literary magazines and reviews from here to Japan and many places in-between! He was a shortlisted candidate for the Hennessy Prize in 1999. He has an MA in Creative Writing, and his first collection *Shaking the Moon* (Flambard/Black Mountain) will be published shortly.

Ted McNulty was a journalist and poet who moved to Ireland in 1990. In 1991 he won the double Tribune Hennessy Awards for New Poet of the Year and New Writer of the Year. His published collections include *Rough Landings* (1992) and *On the Block* (1995). He died in 1998.

Padraig Moran was shortlisted for the Hennessy Tribune Award in 1990. His work has been published in most of the recognised Irish outlets: *Cyphers, The Honest Ulsterman, Force 10, Poetry Ireland Review, Windows, Cuirt, New Irish Writing* and *The Irish Times*. His work also featured in the inaugural *Forward* anthology.

Amanda Norton Unfortunately we were unable to gather biographical details for Amanda.

Carl O'Brien, originally from Killarney, now lives and works in Cork. He is an archivist and historian and teaches in North Monastery CBS.

Eugene O'Connell was born in Kiskeam in North Cork. His poetry has been published in magazines such as: *Poetry Ireland Review, Poetry Scotland* and *The Shop*. He has won many awards including the Eacht Luachra and the Munster Literature Centre's, 'A Sense of Place'. A primary school teacher by profession, he now works as a freelance journalist.

Mary O'Donnell is a novelist, short story writer and poet. Both her poetry and fiction are widely anthologised. She has scripted and presented three series of poetry programmes and is a frequent contributor to national radio. She has published three collections of poetry, a book of short stories and three novels, most recently *The Elysium Testament*.

Bernard O'Donoghue, poet and critic, is the new Director of the Yeats Summer School.

Heather O'Donoghue is a fellow of Oxford University where she teaches Old Norse and Icelandic Literature. She reviews fiction for the *Times Literary Supplement*.

Mary O'Gorman, who grew up in Killarney and now lives in Clonmel, is a previous winner of the *Cork Literary Review*. Her poetry has been widely published: *Poetry Ireland Review, Women's Work, Force 10, Poets for the Millennium, 4 + 4 at 4* (Women artists and poets of the south-east) and elsewhere. She was also shortlisted for the Strokestown Poetry Prize 2000.

Sheila O'Hagan won the Patrick Kavanagh Award for a first manuscript of poetry and the Hennessy Award for New Irish Poet of the Year in 1992. Other awards include the 2000 Strokestown International Poetry Award, the Goldsmith Award for Poetry and several prizes from the Listowel Writers' Week. Her first two collections, *The Peacock's Eye* and *The Troubled House*, were published by Salmon. She is currently working on a third collection of poetry and a collection of short stories.

Nina Quigley, born of Irish-Italian parentage and living in Inishowen, Donegal, has been writing with the 'Shy Wolf Collective' in Derry since 1997. She has been published in magazines such as *Poetry Ireland Review*, *The Honest Ulsterman*, and *Force 10* and has won many prizes for her work. Her first collection of poetry, *Legacy*, a Lapwing poetry pamphlet, is due out soon.

Alice Taylor was born in Newmarket, and now lives in Innishannon. She has written six non-fiction books including *To School Through the Fields*; two volumes of poetry, three children's books and two novels, the second of which, *Across the River*, has just been published. Her work has been translated into German, Polish, Japanese and Dutch.

Margaret Toppin, a retired nurse originally from Clare, has been a member of Dublin's 'Fountain Writers' Group' for over ten years. She has been published in many publications including *Women's Work 1990 –1999*, *Reality*, *Haiku Spirit*, *Riposte*, *Poetry Ireland Review* and *Reach*. She has received prizes for her work from Syllables, *Cuirt*, South Tipperary Arts Festival, Jonathan Swift and the Scottish International Open Poetry Competition. Her first collection *African Violets* was published in 1995.

John Wakeman moved to Ireland from his native London four years ago. Former editor of *The Rialto* in London, he recently founded the poetry magazine, *The Shop*. He has won numerous prizes for his work and has been widely published, including his own collection, *A Room for Doubt*. He was recently featured on the Lyric FM programme, *The Quiet Quarter*, where he gave a series of talks on the subject of Silence.

William Wall is a poet and novelist. His novel, *Alice Falling* was published by Sceptre in February 2000.

Liz Willows, poet, essayist and critic. Her work has appeared in *Northern Star*, *Leeds Other Paper*, *Gay Community News* and *The Common Thread* among others. Her first collection: *If this is Armageddon – it's very pretty* was published in March 2000.

Some other titles from
bradshaw books

bradshaw **b**ooks

Order Form

Name: ————————————————————

Address: ————————————————————

————————————————————

————————————————————

Tel: ————————————————————

Fax: ————————————————————

E-mail: ————————————————————

Title/s: ————————————————————

————————————————————

Number of copies: ————————————————————

Please return to

bradshaw **b**ooks, Tigh Filí, MacCurtain St, Cork.

Tel: 353 21 4509274

Fax: 353 21 4551617

E-mail: admin@cwpc.ie

See our complete list of publications on our
website at http://www.tighfili.com